2,001
Most Useful
SPANISH
Words

Pablo García Loaeza, Ph.D.

DOVER PUBLICATIONS, INC.
Mineola, New York

Bibliographical Note

2,001 Most Useful Spanish Words is a new work, first published by
Dover Publications, Inc., in 2010.

Library of Congress Cataloging-in-Publication Data

Loaeza, Pablo García, 1972–
    2,001 most useful Spanish words / Pablo García Loaeza.
        p. cm.—(Dover Language Guides)
    ISBN-13: 978-0-486-47616-2
    ISBN-10: 0-486-47616-2
        1. Spanish language—Vocabulary.   2. Spanish language—
Usage.   3. Spanish language—Grammar.   I. Title.   II. Title:
Two thousand and one most useful Spanish words.
PC4445L63 2010
468.2'421—dc22

                                                            2010018978

Manufactured in the United States by Courier Corporation
47616201
www.doverpublications.com

Contents

Introduction

This book contains well over two thousand useful Spanish words for general communication and everyday situations. It was designed as a self-teaching tool that can also be used for reference and review. In the first section of the book each alphabetically-ordered word entry includes a sentence in Spanish (and its English translation) that shows how a word might be used. An m. or an f. after a noun indicates whether it is masculine or feminine; the abbreviation pl. stands for plural. Many of the entries include a noun or adjective in parentheses to show the versatility of a specific word. In the second part of the book you will find over four hundred words grouped by categories. These are very common words whose context is self-evident such as numbers, colors, stores, and days of the week; they are not repeated in the alphabetical section. The book takes into account Spanish dialectical variation by including words used in Spain (Sp.) and Latin America, Mexico, Argentina (L. Am., Mex., Arg., etc.).

Vocabulary is best acquired in context and through frequent repetition. When you study the words in this book, picture yourself in the situations in which you might use them. The sentences provided will help you to imagine an appropriate context. Say them out loud to practice hearing and producing the sounds of Spanish. The more familiar they become, the easier it will be for you to understand and be understood when speaking with others. Use the words you learn as often as you can so that they "stick" and become your own.

The illustrative sentences are deliberately simple. As you study a word in a sentence, look at the words around it to discover the way Spanish is structured. In time, you will learn to recognize sever basic structures and rely increasingly less on the English translati After a while, cover the English sentences with a sheet of pape to figure out the meaning of the Spanish sentences on your ov then uncover the English version to check for accuracy. W practice you will find that your translation is correct more not. Certain sentences are organized in small clusters o ring themes. Try reading several sentences at a time t sketches and look for several storylines spread throughout the book which will help you remember the vocabulary as you learn it. (Hint: keep an eye out for my uncle's vegetable garden.)

The Spanish Grammar Primer at the end of the book offers some pointers which you might want to consider as you develop your Spanish vocabulary. Besides vocabulary-building tips and verb conjugation tables, it contains useful information about nouns, pronouns, and prepositions. While practice is always the best way to master a language, many people may find Dover's *Essential Spanish Grammar* (0-486-20780-3) helpful. Likewise, the *1001 Easy Spanish Phrases* (0-486-47619-7), also published by Dover, is a useful complement for increasing your dexterity in Spanish.

A Note on Spanish Dialects

As with English, there are many regional dialects of Spanish. They may vary in pronunciation, vocabulary, and syntax but they are all mutually intelligible.

For instance, in the Castile region of Spain a "c" before an "e" or an "i" sounds like "th" in English and the letter "s" is pronounced like "sh." On the other hand, people in the south of Spain and in Latin America, generally make the letter "c" (before "e" or "i"), the letter "s," and even the letter "z" all sound like the "s" in "soup." Caribbean Spanish tends to drop a "d" between two vowels at the end of some words, as well as a final "s" so that *cansados* (tired, m. pl.) becomes *cansao*. Likewise, in many South-American countries the word for cake is *torta*, whereas in Mexico it is *pastel*. In Latin America a computer is called *una computadora* while in Spain it is referred to as *un ordenador*. Nevertheless, a Spaniard, a Mexican, a Chilean, and a Dominican can engage in conversation without impediment.

When Spanish is learned as a second language the choice of dialect can depend on personal interest and circumstance. For example, someone traveling to Spain might prefer to become familiar with the Castilian dialect, while someone spending time in a Latin American country will pick up the local accent and lingo. The best investment for a beginner studying stateside is to practice a "neutral" kind of Spanish: all the syllables in a word should be pronounced clearly, using the standard word-stress rules (see below). Once you know the basic rules, a little practice makes it easy to compensate for dialectical differences. Remember also that the most useful words, such as *por favor* and *gracias*, are the same throughout the Spanish-speaking world.

Unlike English—in which the same word may be written one way in Britain (colour, dialogue, emphasise, gaol) and another in the United States (color, dialog, emphasize, jail)—all Spanish dialects use the same written standard.

Spanish Pronunciation Guide

Vowels

Spanish only has five vowel sounds (English has over 15!) which correspond to the five vowel letters, regardless of their position in a word. There are no silent vowels in Spanish. The five vowel sounds in Spanish are:

a as in dr**a**ma	*Habla a la casa blanca.*	Call the White House.
e as in b**e**t	*Él es el rebelde René Pérez.*	He is the rebel René Pérez.
i as in d**ee**p	*Sí, viví sin ti.*	Yes, I lived without you.
o as in c**o**at	*Los locos no son tontos.*	Crazy people aren't dumb.
u as in l**oo**p	*Fui a un club nocturno.*	I went to a nightclub.

The semi-consonant **y** is pronounced like **i** [ee] when used as a conjunction: Pedro **y** María (*Pedro* **and** María); its sound softens next to a vowel (as in **ye**llow): Juan y **yo** somos muy buenos amigos (*Juan and I are very good friends*).

Consonants

Spanish has basically the same consonant sounds as English. However, there are a few particulars to keep in mind:

b and **v** are very often pronounced the same way as in "**b**ee."
c (soft), **s**, and **z** vary in pronunciation in some Spanish dialects. However, in all but the rarest cases, they can all be pronounced like the **s** in "**s**oft" without risk of confusion.
g is hard as in **g**ood before **a**, **o**, and **u**, but soft as the **h** in ho⟍ before **e** or **i**.
gu is used before **e** and **i** to represent a soft **g** sound as in goo⟍ that here the **u** does not function as a vowel; **gu** is a di⟍ which two letters represent a single sound as in **th**e)
h is always mute as in **h**erbs.
j is pronounced like the **h** in **h**orse.

ll is always pronounced like **y** as in **y**ellow.

ñ represents a particular sound which resembles the **ny** combination found in ca**ny**on or bar**ny**ard.

qu is used before **e** and **i** to represent a hard **c** sound as in **c**at (see **gu** above)

r at the beginning of a word is trilled.

rr represents a trill in the middle of a word.

Stress and written accents

Spanish words tend to have two or more syllables; when they are pronounced one syllable always sounds a little bit louder than the others. The stressed syllable is either the last, the next to last (most often), or the second to last syllable (least often). Word stress in Spanish is determined by two simple rules:

1. Words that end in a **vowel, n,** or **s** are generally pronounced stressing the **next to last syllable**:
   Vent**a**na (*window*), **bar**co (*boat*), pa**lab**ras (*words*), tú **can**tas (*you sing*), ellos **com**en (*they eat*)
2. Words which end in a **consonant** other than **n** or **s** are generally stressed on the **last syllable**:
   pa**pel** (*paper*), fe**liz** (*happy*), acti**tud** (*attitude*), can**tar** (*to sing*), com**er** (*to eat*)

Written accent marks indicate a stress where you wouldn't normally expect it:
can**ción** (*song*), él can**tó** (*he sang*),* **lá**piz (*pencil*), a**zú**car (*sugar*), mur**cié**lago (*bat*)[†], **cír**culo (*circle*)

---

*Note the difference with yo **can**to (*I sing*): a change in stress can significantly change the meaning of a word or even a whole sentence.
[†]Repeating the word **murciélago** out loud is a good way to practice pronunciation: as all five vowel sounds and distinctive stress.

Alphabetical Section

A

a (tiempo, veces)   *to, on time, some times*
A veces salgo a comer y trato de llegar a tiempo.
Sometimes I go out to eat and I try to be on time.

a bordo   *on board*
Bienvenidos a bordo.
Welcome on board.

a menudo   *often*
Lavo mi ropa a menudo.
I wash my clothes often.

a través   *across, through*
Muchas cosas han cambiado a través de los años.
Many things have changed through the years.

abajo (de)   *under, down*
La maleta está abajo.
The suitcase is downstairs.

abierto/-a   *open*
La farmacia está abierta.
The drugstore is open.

abogado/-a m./f.   *lawyer*
Voy a llamar a un abogado.
I am going to call a lawyer.

aborto (natural) m.   *abortion, miscarriage*
El aborto es un asunto polémico.
Abortion is a controversial subject.

abrazar   *to hug, to embrace*
En México, los amigos se abrazan al saludarse.
In Mexico, friends hug each other when they meet.

abrelatas m.   *can opener*
Nunca hay un abrelatas cuando lo necesitas.
There's never a can opener when you need it.

abridor m.   *bottle opener*
Necesito un abridor para abrir esta botella.
I need a bottle opener to open this bottle.

aburrido/-a   *bored, boring, dull*
Esta película es muy aburrida.
This movie is very boring.

aburrir(se)   *to bore, to get bored*
A menudo me aburro los domingos.
Often, I get bored on Sundays.

acabar   *to finish*
Acaba tu tarea antes de irte.
Finish your homework before you leave.

acampar   *to camp*
¿Hay un lugar donde acampar por aquí?
Is there a place to camp around here?

accidente m.   *accident*
Por suerte, el accidente no fue grave.
Luckily, the accident wasn't serious.

aceptar   *to accept*
¿Aceptan tarjetas de crédito?
Do you accept credit cards?

acera f.   *sidewalk*
Es más seguro caminar por la acera.
It's safer to walk on the sidewalk.

acompañante m. & f.   *companion*
¿Cómo se llama tu acompañante?
What's your companion's name?

acompañar   *to accompany*
¿Me acompañas al parque?
Will you accompany me to the park?

consejar   *to advise, to recommend*
Te aconsejo usar crema solar en la playa.
I recommend you use sunscreen at the beach.

acordarse   *to remember*
Siempre me acordaré de ti.
I will always remember you.

acostar(se)   *to lay down, to go to bed*
Es bueno acostarse temprano.
It's good to go to bed early.

actual   *current*
La política siempre es un tema actual.
Politics is always a current topic.

actuar   *to act*
Piensa, y después actúa.
Think, and then act.

acuario m.   *aquarium*
Vi tiburones en el acuario.
I saw sharks at the aquarium.

acuerdo m.   *agreement*
Todos firmaron el acuerdo.
Everyone signed the agreement.

adaptador m.   *adaptor*
¿Dónde puedo comprar un adaptador de corriente?
Where can I buy a power adaptor?

adelante   *forward*
¡Vamos adelante!
Let's go forward!

adentro m.   *inside, within*
Vamos adentro.
Let's go inside.

adicto/-a   *addicted*
No es bueno ser adicto a nada.
It's not good to be addicted to anything.

adiós   *good-bye*
Es triste tener que decir adiós.
It's sad to have to say good-bye.

adivinar   *to guess*
Si quieres que te lo dé, adivina lo que es.
If you want me to give it to you, guess what it is.

administrar   *to manage*
Necesito administrar mejor mi dinero.
I need to manage my money better.

admirar   *to admire*
Quiero admirar la vista desde aquí.
I want to admire the view from here.

admitir   *to admit*
Admito que me equivoqué.
I admit I was wrong.

adquirir   *to get, to acquire, to buy*
¿Dónde puedo adquirir los boletos?
Where can I get the tickets?

adrede   *on purpose, deliberately*
¿Hiciste eso adrede?
Did you do that on purpose?

aduana f.   *customs*
Al llegar, debemos pasar por la aduana.
On arrival, we have to go through customs.

advertir   *to warn*
Le advertí que no lo hiciera.
I warned him not to do it.

aerolínea f.   *airline*
Siempre viajamos por la misma aerolínea.
We always travel with the same airline.

aeropuerto m.   *airport*
El aeropuerto está cerca de la ciudad.
The airport is near the city.

afectar   *to affect, to upset*
Las malas noticias me afectaron mucho.
The bad news upset me a lot.

afecto m.   *affection*
Los regalos son una forma de mostrar afecto.
Presents are a way to show affection.

afeitar(se)   *to shave*
Antes de bañarme me afeito.
Before taking a bath, I shave.

aficionado m.   *fan, amateur*
Soy un aficionado del fútbol americano.
I am a fan of football.

afilado/-a   *sharp*
Este cuchillo no está muy afilado.
This knife is not very sharp.

afortunadamente   *fortunately*
Afortunadamente, nadie se lastimó.
Fortunately, no one got hurt.

afuera   *outside*
¿Hace frío afuera?
Is it cold outside?

agencia (de viajes) f.   *(travel) agency*
¿Sabe dónde está la agencia de viajes más cercana?
Do you know where the nearest travel agency is?

agente (de viajes) m. & f.   *(travel) agent*
Necesitamos un buen agente de viajes.
We need a good travel agent.

agradable   *pleasant*
Las noches de verano son muy agradables aquí.
Summer nights are very pleasant here.

agradecer   *to thank*
Le agradezco su amabilidad.
I thank you for your kindness.

agradecido/-a   *grateful*
Estoy muy agradecido por su ayuda.
I am very grateful for your help.

agregar   *to add*
¿Me puede agregar a la lista?
Can you add me to the list?

agresivo/-a   *aggressive*
El sol tropical puede ser agresivo.
The tropical sun can be aggressive.

aguja f.   *needle*
Necesito aguja e hilo para arreglar mi vestido.
I need needle and thread to mend my dress.

ahogar(se)   *to drown, to choke*
Se ahogó por nadar en el mar en la noche.
He drowned swimming in the sea at night.

ahora (mismo)   *right now*
Debemos salir ahora mismo para llegar a tiempo.
We must leave right now to be on time.

ahorrar   *to save*
Queremos ahorrar dinero.
We want to save money.

aire (acondicionado) m.   *air (conditioning)*
¿Tiene aire acondicionado la habitación?
Does the room have air conditioning?

ajedrez m.   *chess*
¿Sabes jugar ajedrez?
Do you know how to play chess?

al contado   *in cash*
Prefiero pagar al contado.
I prefer to pay in cash.

al fin   *finally*
Nos perdimos, pero al fin llegamos.
We got lost, but we finally made it.

al lado de   *next to*
Mi oficina está al lado de la tuya.
My office is next to yours.

albergue (juvenil) m.   *(youth) hostel*
Estamos buscando un albergue juvenil.
We are looking for a youth hostel.

alcohol m.   *alcohol*
En muchos países se puede beber alcohol a los dieciocho años.
In many countries one can drink alcohol at eighteen.

alcohólico/-a   *alcoholic*
¿Venden bebidas alcohólicas aquí?
Do you sell alcoholic drinks here?

alegrar(se)   *to make someone happy*
Me alegra verte.
I'm happy to see you.

alegre   *cheerful*
Juan es una persona alegre.
Juan is a cheerful person.

alegría f.   *cheerfulness*
Me gusta la alegría de las fiestas decembrinas.
I like the cheerfulness of the winter holidays.

alérgico/-a   *allergic*
Soy alérgico a los camarones.
I am allergic to shrimp.

alfiler m.   *pin*
Esto no se puede arreglar con un alfiler.
This can't be fixed with a pin.

alfombra f.   *carpet*
¡Que bonita alfombra!
What a nice carpet!

algo   *something*
¿Quieres algo de comer?
Do you want something to eat?

algodón m.   *cotton*
Quiero comprar unas camisas de algodón.
I want to buy some cotton shirts.

alguien   *somebody, someone*
¿Me llamó alguien por teléfono?
Did someone call me on the phone?

algún, alguno/-a(s)   *some*
A algunas personas no les gusta viajar.
Some people don't like to travel.

alimentar(se)   *to feed, to eat*
Es necesario alimentarse bien para tener energía.
It is necessary to eat well to have energy.

aliviar   *to relieve, to alleviate*
¿Quieres algo para aliviar el dolor?
Do you want something to relieve the pain?

alivio m.   *relief*
Fue un alivio alcanzar el vuelo.
It was a relief to catch the flight.

allí/allá   *there/over there*
¿Qué es eso que está allá?
What's that over there?

almacén m.   *warehouse, store*
¿Me puede decir donde hay un almacén de comida?
Can you tell me where there's a grocery store?

almohada f.   *pillow*
Tengo dos almohadas en mi cama.
I have two pillows on my bed.

almorzar   *to have lunch*
¿Me puede recomendar un lugar para almorzar?
Can you recommend a place to have lunch?

alojamiento m.   *lodging*
Estoy buscando alojamiento para mis vacaciones.
I am looking for lodging for my vacation.

alojar(se)   *to lodge (at a hotel)*
Nos alojaremos aquí esta noche.
We will lodge/stay here tonight.

alquilar   *to rent*
Mi cuñado quiere alquilar una casa en Acapulco.
My brother-in-law wants to rent a house in Acapulco.

alquiler m.   *rent*
¿Es muy caro el alquiler de este departamento?
Is this apartment's rent very expensive?

alrededores m. pl.   *outskirts*
Los alrededores de la ciudad no son muy interesantes.
The outskirts of the city are not very interesting.

altar   *altar*
Los altares barrocos suelen ser espectaculares.
Baroque altars are often spectacular.

alto   *stop*
Una luz roja significa hacer un alto
A red light means to stop.

alto/-a   *tall, high*
¡Qué montaña tan alta!
What a tall mountain!

altura f.   *height*
Las alturas me dan miedo.
Heights scare me.

alucinar   *to hallucinate*
Debes estar alucinando.
You must be hallucinating.

alumno/-a m./f.   *student, pupil*
Soy alumno en la universidad.
I am a student at the university.

amabilidad f.   *kindness*
La amabilidad es una virtud.
Kindness is a virtue.

amable   *kind*
Miguel es una persona muy amable.
Miguel is a very kind person.

amar(se)   *to love (each other)*
Yo te amo y tú amas la música.
I love you and you love music.

amante m. & f.   *lover*
Jorge es un amante de la música.
Jorge is a music lover.

ambos   *both*
Ambos trenes llegaron al mismo tiempo.
Both trains arrived at the same time.

ambulancia f.   *ambulance*
¡Alguien llame una ambulancia!
Somebody call an ambulance!

amenaza f.   *threat*
Actualmente hay muchas amenazas para la vida en este planeta.
Currently there are many threats to life on this planet.

amanecer   *(to) dawn*
Me encanta ver el amanecer junto al mar.
I love watching the dawn by the sea.

amigo/-a m./f.   *friend*
María es una buena amiga mía.
Maria is a good friend of mine.

amistad f.   *friendship*
La amistad es verdaderamente una gran cosa.
Friendship is truly a great thing.

amistoso/-a   *friendly*
El empleado de la tienda fue muy amistoso
The store clerk was very friendly.

amor m.   *love*
El amor verdadero es difícil de encontrar.
True love is hard to find.

analista (de sistemas)   *(systems) analyst*
Marcos es analista de sistemas.
Marcos is a systems analyst.

analizar   *to analyze*
Debemos analizar el problema.
We must analyze the problem.

ancho/-a   *wide, broad*
El río amazonas es muy ancho.
The Amazon River is very wide.

anciano/-a m./f.   *elderly, old man/woman*
Este asiento está reservado para los ancianos.
This seat is reserved for the elderly.

andar   *to go, to walk*
Me gustaría andar por el centro de la ciudad.
I would like to walk around downtown.

andar en bicicleta   *to ride a bicycle*
Todo mundo sabe andar en bicicleta.
Everybody knows how to ride a bike.

andén m.   *train platform*
Los pasajeros esperan el tren en el andén.
The passengers wait for the train on the platform.

anfitrión(a) m./f.   *host*
Gracias por ser un excelente anfitrión
Thank you for being an excellent host.

anillo m.   *ring*
¡No puedo encontrar mi anillo de boda!
I can't find my wedding ring!

anotar   *to make note*
¿Anotaste la dirección del albergue?
Did you make note of the hostel address?

ansioso/-a   *anxious*
Estoy ansioso por terminar este proyecto.
I'm anxious to finish this project.

anteojos m. pl.   *eyeglasses*
No puedo ver nada sin mis anteojos.
I cannot see a thing without my eyeglasses.

anterior   *the one before, the previous one*
Este libro es mejor que el anterior.
This book is better than the previous one.

antes   *before*
Es importante lavarse las manos antes de comer.
It's important to wash one's hands before eating.

antigüedad f.   *antique*
Eso no es una antigüedad, es basura.
That's not an antique, it's junk.

antiguo/-a   *ancient/old*
La cultura azteca es muy antigua.
Aztec culture is very old.

antipático/-a   *unfriendly, unkind*
El mesero que nos atendió era muy antipático.
The waiter who took care of us was very unfriendly.

anular   *to cancel*
Anulé mi cita con el doctor.
I canceled my doctor's appointment.

anuncio m.   *advertisement*
Hay anuncios por todas partes.
There are advertisements everywhere.

apagar   *to turn off*
Por favor, apaga el radio.
Please, turn off the radio.

aparador m.   *store window*
Me gusta ir al centro de la ciudad para ver aparadores.
I like to go downtown to see the store windows.

aparecer *to appear*
Las estrellas aparecieron en el cielo.
The stars appeared in the sky.

apellido m. *family name, last name*
Mi apellido es Bond.
My last name is Bond.

apenado/-a *sorry, ashamed, embarrassed*
Estoy muy apenado por haber llegado tarde.
I am very sorry for being late.

aplaudir *to applaud*
El público aplaudió mucho al final de la función.
The audience applauded a lot at the end of the show.

apodo m. *nickname*
Algunos apodos son descriptivos.
Some nicknames are descriptive.

apoyar(se) *to lean on/support*
Puedes apoyarte en mí.
You can lean on me.

aprender (de memoria) *to learn (by heart)*
Quiero aprender a bailar tango.
I want to learn to dance the tango.

apresurar(se) *to hurry*
Apresúrate, se nos hace tarde.
Hurry up, it's getting late.

apretado/-a *tight*
Estos zapatos se sienten muy apretados.
These shoes feel very tight.

aprovechar *to take advantage of*
Quiero aprovechar la luz para tomar unas fotos.
I want to take advantage of the light to take some pictures.

apuesta f. *bet*
¿Es legal hacer apuestas sobre el juego?
Is it legal to make bets on the game?

apuntar *to point*
Una brújula siempre apunta al norte.
A compass always points north.

aquí/acá   *here/over here*
¡Ven para acá ahora mismo!
Come over here right now!

árbol m.   *tree*
Quiero descansar a la sombra de un árbol.
I want to rest under the shade of a tree.

arbusto m.   *bush*
El sendero está atrás de aquellos arbustos.
The path is behind those bushes.

archivo m.   *file*
Los archivos están guardados en el disco duro de mi
   computadora.
The files are stored on the hard drive of my computer.

arco (iris) m.   *arch, bow, rainbow*
Después de la tormenta vimos un arco iris.
After the storm we saw a rainbow.

arder   *to burn*
Me arde la piel porque no me puse crema solar.
My skin burns because I didn't put on sunscreen.

arena f.   *sand*
¿Quieres construir un castillo de arena?
Do you want to build a sand castle?

armario m.   *closet, wardrobe*
Este departamento tiene muchos armarios.
This apartment has a lot of closets.

arquitectura f.   *architecture*
Vale la pena visitar Sevilla por su arquitectura.
Seville is worth visiting for its architecture.

arreglar   *to fix, to arrange*
¿Quién nos puede arreglar el auto?
Who can fix our car for us?

arreglo m.   *arrangement, repair*
Es un buen arreglo.
It is a good arrangement.

arrendar   *to rent*
Queremos arrendar unas bicicletas.
We want to rent some bikes.

arriba   *up*
Mira hacia arriba.
Look up.

arriesgar(se)   *to risk*
El que apuesta arriesga su dinero.
The one who bets risks his money.

arroyo m.   *stream*
Es agradable caminar junto al arroyo.
It is nice to walk by the stream.

arruinar   *to ruin, to spoil*
La lluvia arruinó la excursión.
The rain ruined the outing.

artesanía f.   *(hand) crafts*
México es muy conocido por sus artesanías.
Mexico is well-known for its crafts.

asar   *to roast*
¿Vamos a asar el pollo?
Will we roast the chicken?

ascensor m.   *elevator*
El edificio tiene dos ascensores.
The building has two elevators.

asco m.   *disgust*
Siento asco por ese mal olor.
That bad smell disgusts me.

asegurar(se)   *to insure, to secure, to make sure*
Asegúrate de no olvidar nada.
Make sure you're not forgetting anything.

asesinar   *to murder*
¿Quién asesinó al presidente?
Who murdered the president?

asesinato m.   *murder*
El asesinato es un crimen que se castiga severamente.
Murder is a crime that is severely punished.

asfixiar(se)   *to choke*
Demasiado humo puede asfixiar a alguien.
Too much smoke can choke someone.

así   *thus, this way*
Mira, es mejor hacerlo así.
Look, it's better to do it this way.

asiento (para bebé) m.   *(child) seat*
¿Está ocupado este asiento?
Is this seat taken?

asistir (a)   *to attend*
Quiero asistir al concierto esta noche.
I want to attend the concert tonight.

asolearse   *to sunbathe*
Es malo para la piel asolearse por mucho tiempo.
It is bad for the skin to sunbathe for a long time.

asombroso/-a   *amazing*
El espectáculo fue asombroso.
The show was amazing.

astilla f.   *splinter*
Una astilla puede ser muy incómoda.
A splinter can be very uncomfortable.

asunto m.   *matter, subject*
El calentamiento global es un asunto importante.
Global warming is an important matter.

asustar(se)   *to scare, to get scared, be surprised, be startled*
Me asusté cuando me dijo el precio del vestido.
I was surprised when she told me the price of the dress.

atar   *to tie*
Ata la cuerda al poste para colgar la hamaca.
Tie the rope to the post to hang up the hammock.

atención f.   *attention*
¿Estás prestando atención?
Are you paying attention?

atender   *to tend to, to take care of*
Un buen médico atiende a sus pacientes.
A good doctor takes care of his patients.

atraer   *to attract*
Ser descortés atrae problemas.
Being impolite attracts trouble.

atrapar   *to catch*
Atrapa la pelota.
Catch the ball.

atrás   *behind*
Da un paso atrás.
Take a step back.

atreverse   *to dare*
No me atrevo a saltar en paracaídas.
I don't dare parachute jump.

atropellar   *to run over*
Cruza la calle con cuidado para evitar que te atropellen.
Cross the street carefully to avoid getting run over.

audífonos m. pl.   *earphones*
Quítate los audífonos para poder oír lo que te estoy diciendo.
Take off your earphones so you can hear what I'm telling you.

aumentar   *to increase*
El precio del dólar ha aumentado recientemente.
The (currency) exchange rate has increased recently.

aún   *yet, still*
El tren no ha llegado aún.
The train has not arrived yet.

aunque   *although, even though*
La excursión tuvo lugar aunque estaba lloviendo.
The excursion took place even though it was raining.

ausencia f.   *absence*
Nadie notó mi ausencia.
Nobody noticed my absence.

autobús m.   *bus*
¿Se puede llegar allá en autobús?
Can you get there by bus?

automóvil m.   *car, automobile*
Me gustaría rentar un automóvil.
I would like to rent a car.

autopista f.   *highway*
Me gustan más los caminos que las autopistas.
I like roads more than highways.

autoridad f.   *authority*
Usted no tiene la autoridad para hacer esto.
You don't have the authority to do this.

avenida f.   *avenue*
Hay muchas tiendas en la avenida principal.
There are a lot of stores on the main avenue.

avergonzado/-a   *ashamed, embarrassed*
Me siento muy avergonzado.
I feel very embarrassed.

averiado/-a   *out of order, broken down*
Tendremos que usar las escaleras porque el ascensor está
    averiado.
We'll have to use the stairs because the elevator is out of order.

averiguar   *to find out*
Me gustaría averiguar a qué hora abre el museo.
I would like to find out what time the museum opens.

avión m.   *airplane*
Viajaré a España en avión.
I will travel to Spain by airplane.

avisar   *to inform, to warn*
Pedro me avisó que llegaría tarde.
Pedro informed me that he would be late.

aviso m.   *warning, sign*
Debemos hacer caso de los avisos.
We must pay attention to the signs.

ayuda f.   *help*
Necesito tu ayuda.
I need your help.

ayudar   *to help*
Por favor ayúdame.
Please help me.

B

bahía f.   *bay*
La bahía de Acapulco es la más bella del mundo.
The Bay of Acapulco is the most beautiful in the world.

bailar   *to dance*
¿Quiere bailar?
Would you like to dance?

bailarín(a) m./f.   *dancer*
Usted es un buen bailarín.
You are a good dancer.

baile m.   *dance*
México tiene muchos bailes folklóricos.
Mexico has many folk dances.

bajada f.   *descent*
Ten cuidado en la bajada.
Be careful on the descent.

bajar   *to lower, to go down, to descend*
¡Bajen a cenar!
Come down to eat dinner!

bajo/-a   *low*
¿Cuál es el precio más bajo por este anillo?
What is the lowest price for this ring?

bañar(se)   *to bathe, to take a bath*
Me baño todos los días.
I take a bath every day.

banco/a m./f.   *bank/stool, bench*
Esperaré en la banca mientras tú vas al banco.
I will wait on the bench while you go to the bank.

bandeja f.   *tray*
Nos sirvieron el desayuno en bandejas de plata.
They served us breakfast on silver trays.

bandera f.   *flag*
¿Cuáles son los colores de la bandera nacional de este país?
What are the colors of this country's national flag?

bañera f.   *bathtub*
Los buenos hoteles tienen bañeras en los cuartos de baño.
Good hotels have bathtubs in the bathrooms.

baño m.   *bathroom*
El baño en este departamento es muy pequeño.
The bathroom in this apartment is very small.

banquero m. & f.   *banker*
Los banqueros son muy ricos.
Bankers are very rich.

barato/-a   *cheap*
Compré un reloj muy barato; sólo me costó $10 dólares.
I bought a very cheap watch; it was only $10 dollars.

barco (de vela) m.   *(sail) boat, ship*
Quiero navegar en un barco de vela.
I want to sail in a sailboat.

barman m. & f.   *bartender*
El barman nos regaló los tragos.
The bartender gave us our drinks for free.

barrio m.   *neighborhood*
Este es un barrio muy agradable.
This is a very nice neighborhood.

base (de datos) f.   *(data)base*
En cualquier negocio es una buena idea tener una base de datos.
In any business it is a good idea to have a database.

bastante   *enough*
¿Dormiste bastante anoche?
Did you sleep enough last night?

basura f.   *garbage, trash*
La basura es un gran problema en las ciudades grandes.
Garbage is a big problem in big cities.

basurero m.   *trash bin/can/dumpsters*
Algunos barrios no tienen suficientes basureros.
Some neighborhoods don't have enough trash bins.

batería f.   *(car) battery/drum set*
Creo que esta linterna necesita baterías.
I think this flashlight needs batteries.

batido m.   *blended, milkshake*
Quiero un batido de plátano.
I want a banana milkshake.

bebé m. & f.   *baby*
¡Qué lindo bebé!
What a cute baby!

beber   *to drink*
Me gusta beber vino tinto.
I like to drink red wine.

belleza f.   *beauty*
La belleza de este lugar es impresionante.
The beauty of this place is impressive.

besar   *to kiss*
¡Bésame!
Kiss me!

beso m.   *kiss*
En muchos países la gente se saluda con un beso.
In many countries people greet each other with a kiss.

biblia f.   *bible*
Suele haber una biblia en los cuartos de hotel.
There's usually a bible in hotel rooms.

biblioteca f.   *library*
Visito la biblioteca todos los días.
I visit the library every day.

bicicleta (de montaña, de carreras) f.   *(mountain, racing) bicycle*
La bicicleta de montaña y la de carreras son muy diferentes.
A mountain bicycle and a racing bicycle are very different.

bien (hecho)   *well (done)*
Este es un trabajo bien hecho.
This is a job well done.

bienes m. pl.   *goods*
Debes cuidar tus bienes.
You must take care of your goods.

bienestar m.   *well-being*
La salud es importante para el bienestar de una persona.
Health is important for a person's well-being.

bienvenido/-a   *welcome*
¡Bienvenidos a nuestra casa!
Welcome to our house!

bilingüe   *bilingual*
Ser bilingüe es una gran ventaja.
Being bilingual is a great advantage.

billete m.   *banknote/ticket*
Compraré los billetes para el teatro esta tarde.
I will buy the tickets for the theater this evening.

billetera f.   *wallet*
Alguien me robó mi billetera.
Somebody stole my wallet.

blando/-a   *soft*
Este sillón es muy blando.
This couch is very soft.

boda f.   *wedding*
La boda será en la iglesia.
The wedding will be at the church.

bodega f.   *storage room/cellar*
Guardo la aspiradora en la bodega.
I keep the vacuum cleaner in the storage room.

boleto (de ida y vuelta) m.   *(round trip) ticket*
Compraré los boletos para la opera mañana en la mañana.
I will buy the tickets for the opera tomorrow morning.

bolígrafo m.   *ballpoint pen*
Préstame tu bolígrafo para firmar estos documentos.
Lend me your ballpoint pen to sign these documents.

bolsa f.   *bag, purse*
No guardes tu pasaporte en tu bolsa.
Don't keep your passport in your bag.

bolso m.   *purse (Sp.)*
Se me olvidó mi bolso.
I forgot my purse.

bombero m. & f.   *fireman*
¡Llamen a los bomberos!
Call the firemen!

bombilla (eléctrica) f.   *light bulb*
Edison inventó la bombilla eléctrica.
Edison invented the light bulb.

bondad f.   *goodness, kindness*
La bondad es mejor que la inteligencia.
Goodness is better than intelligence.

bondadoso/-a   *caring*
Luisa es una persona muy bondadosa.
Luisa is a very caring person.

bonito/-a   *pretty*
Laura es una mujer bonita.
Laura is a pretty woman.

borracho/-a   *drunk*
Creo que Antonio está borracho.
I think Antonio is drunk.

borrar   *to erase*
Me gustaría borrar los malos recuerdos.
I would like to erase bad memories.

bosque m.   *forest*
Me perdí en el bosque.
I got lost in the forest.

botella f.   *bottle*
Pásame la botella de vino, por favor.
Pass me the wine bottle, please.

botones m. & f.   *bellhop*
¿Dónde está el botones?
Where's the bellhop?

brillar   *to shine, to glow*
Las estrellas brillan más cerca del mar.
Stars shine more by the sea.

brincar   *to jump*
Brincó desde el acantilado.
He jumped from the cliff.

brindis m.   *toast*
Quiero hacer un brindis.
I want to make a toast.

brisa f.   *breeze*
No hay nada como una brisa tropical.
There is nothing like a tropical breeze.

broma f.   *joke, gag*
No me gustan las bromas.
I don't like practical jokes.

bronceador m.   *tanning lotion*
No olvides llevar bronceador a la playa.
Don't forget to take tanning lotion to the beach.

brujo/-a m./f.   *wizard/witch*
Los brujos y las brujas sólo existen en los cuentos de hadas.
Wizards and witches exist only in fairy tales.

brújula f.   *compass*
Si tuviéramos una brújula no estaríamos tan perdidos.
If we had a compass we wouldn't be so lost.

brumoso/-a   *foggy*
Está brumoso ahora pero más tarde saldrá el sol.
It's foggy now but later the sun will come out.

bucear   *to scuba dive*
Me gustaría aprender a bucear.
I would like to learn to scuba dive.

buceo m.   *scuba diving*
El arrecife de coral es el mejor lugar para el buceo.
The coral reef is the best place for scuba diving.

bueno/-a, buen (rato)   *good (time)*
Pasé algunos buenos ratos en Sevilla.
I had some good times in Seville.

buscar   *to look for*
Estoy buscando un restaurante barato.
I am looking for a cheap restaurant.

buzón m.   *mailbox*
¿Dónde hay un buzón?
Where is there a mailbox?

C

caballero m.   *gentleman*
Ernesto es un verdadero caballero.
Ernesto is a true gentleman.

cabaña f.   *cabin, shack, hut*
Tengo una cabaña en las montañas.
I have a cabin in the mountains.

caber   *to fit (in)*
Toda esa ropa no va a caber en tu maleta.
All those clothes won't fit in your suitcase.

cabina (de teléfono) f.   *(telephone) booth, cabin*
Estoy buscando una cabina telefónica.
I am looking for a telephone booth.

cabo m.   *cape, end*
Finalmente llegamos al final del camino.
Finally, we got to the end of the road.

cada   *each*
Hay vuelos que salen cada hora.
There are flights leaving each hour.

cadena f.   *chain*
Hagamos una cadena humana.
Let's make a human chain.

caduco/-a   *expired/out-of-date*
Esta medicina está caduca.
This medicine is expired.

caer(se)   *to fall (down)*
Se tropezó y se cayó.
He tripped and fell down.

café m.   *coffee shop/coffee*
Te veré en el café.
I will see you at the coffee shop.

cafetera f.   *coffee pot*
Pon el café en la cafetera.
Put the coffee in the coffee pot.

caída f.   *fall*
Por suerte no fue una caída seria.
Luckily it wasn't a serious fall.

caja (de ahorros) f.   *box, savings bank*
Es mejor guardar el dinero en una caja de ahorros que en una caja de zapatos.
It is better to keep money in a savings bank than in a shoe box.

cajero (automático) m.   *cashier, ATM machine*
Paga la cuenta en el cajero.
Pay the bill with the cashier.

cajón m.   *drawer*
Las camisas están en el primer cajón.
The shirts are in the first drawer.

calculadora f.   *calculator*
¿Tienes una calculadora que puedes prestarme?
Do you have a calculator I can borrow?

calefacción (central) f.   *(central) heating*
En los países trópicos, no se necesita calefacción.
In the tropics, central heating is not needed.

calendario m.   *calendar*
Según el calendario, hoy es el primero de enero.
According to the calendar, today is January first.

calentador m.   *heater*
El calentador de agua es eléctrico.
The water heater is electric.

calentar(se)   *to warm, to heat (up)*
Me caliento cerca de la chimenea.
I warm up near the chimney.

calidad f.   *quality*
Estos zapatos son de muy buena calidad.
These shoes are very good quality.

caliente   *hot*
No me gusta la sopa demasiado caliente.
I don't like soup too hot.

callar(se) *to quiet, to be quiet*
Cállate o te callo a la fuerza.
Be quiet or I'll quiet you by force.

calle f. *street*
Es mejor caminar por el lado sombreado de la calle.
It is better to walk on the shady side of the street.

callejón (sin salida) m. *alley, dead end*
Me gustan los callejones de Toledo.
I like the alleys in Toledo.

calmar(se) *to calm (down)*
¡Cálmese!
Calm down!

calor m. *heat, warmth*
Hoy hace mucho calor afuera.
Today it's very hot outside.

calvo/-a *bald*
Creo que me estoy quedando calvo.
I think I'm going bald.

cama (doble) f. *(double) bed*
Quiero una habitación con una cama doble.
I want a room with a double bed.

cámara (fotográfica) f. *camera*
Se me olvidó mi cámara.
I forgot my camera.

camarero/-a m./f. *waiter, waitress*
Camarero, mi cuenta por favor.
Waiter, my check please.

camarote m. *ship's cabin*
Pedí un camarote de segunda clase.
I asked for a second class (ship's) cabin.

cambiar (un cheque) *to change, to exchange, to cash a check*
¿Puede cambiarme este cheque de viajero?
Can you cash this traveler's check for me?

cambio m. *change/cash*
Necesito cambio para dar propinas.
I need change to give tips.

caminar   *to walk*
Me gusta caminar por el parque.
I like to walk through the park.

camino m.   *road*
¿Es este el camino correcto?
Is this the right road?

camión (de bomberos) m.   *(fire) truck*
El camión de bomberos está por llegar.
The fire truck will be here soon.

camisa f.   *shirt*
¿Tiene camisas de algodón?
Do you have cotton shirts?

camiseta f.   *T-shirt, undershirt*
Llevo camiseta en la playa.
I wear a T-shirt at the beach.

camisón m.   *nightgown*
Mi esposa usa camisón para dormir.
My wife wears a nightgown while sleeping.

campana f.   *bell*
La iglesia tiene una campana.
The church has a bell.

campeón(a) m./f.   *champion*
El campeón ganó el torneo otra vez.
The champion won the tournament again.

campesino m.   *farmer*
Los campesinos son muy importantes para la economía.
Farmers are very important for the economy.

campo m.   *field, countryside*
Me gustaría vivir en el campo.
I would like to live in the countryside.

canasta f.   *basket*
No pongas todos tus huevos en una sola canasta.
Don't put all your eggs in one basket.

cáncer m.   *cancer*
Ha habido avances significativos en el tratamiento contra el cáncer.
There have been significant advances in cancer treatment.

canción f.   *song*
Me gustan las canciones tradicionales.
I like traditional songs.

candado m.   *padlock*
La reja está cerrada con un candado.
The grate is locked with a padlock.

candidato/-a m./f.   *candidate*
El candidato popular no siempre gana las elecciones.
The popular candidate doesn't always win the elections.

cansado/-a   *tired*
Estoy muy cansado.
I am very tired.

cansancio m.   *tiredness*
Sentía gran cansancio después de caminar todo el día.
He felt great weariness after walking all day.

cantante m. & f.   *singer*
El cantante dio un buen concierto.
The singer gave a good concert.

cantar   *to sing*
Siempre canto en la regadera.
I always sing in the shower.

cantidad f.   *quantity*
La calidad es mejor que la cantidad.
Quality is better than quantity.

cantimplora f.   *water bottle/canteen*
Es importante llevar una cantimplora a la excursión.
It's important to take a water bottle on the trip.

capa de ozono f.   *ozone layer*
La capa de ozono sigue desapareciendo.
The ozone layer is still disappearing.

capacidad f.   *capability, capacity*
Estoy trabajando al máximo de mi capacidad.
I'm working at my maximum capacity.

capaz   *capable*
Es un hombre muy capaz.
He is a very capable man.

capilla f.   *chapel*
Las capillas rodean la nave principal.
The chapels surround the main nave.

capricho m.   *whim*
Fui a Chile por capricho.
I went to Chile on a whim.

captura de datos f.   *data processing*
Mi amigo tiene un negocio de captura de datos.
My friend has a data-processing business.

carcajada f.   *hard laugh/guffaw*
Es saludable reír a carcajadas de vez en cuando.
It's healthy to have a hard laugh once in a while.

cárcel f.   *jail, prison*
Este hotel solía ser la cárcel de la ciudad.
This hotel used to be the city's jail.

cargar   *to carry/to charge/to load*
No lleves lo que no puedas cargar.
Don't take what you can't carry.

cargo extra m.   *surcharge*
Empaca ligero para evitar cargos extra.
Pack lightly to avoid surcharges.

cariño m.   *affection, fondness*
Siento mucho cariño por mi novia.
I feel a lot of affection for my girlfriend.

cariñoso/-a   *affectionate*
Los perros suelen ser más cariñosos que los gatos.
Dogs are generally more affectionate than cats.

caro/-a   *expensive*
Estos zapatos son demasiado caros.
These shoes are too expensive.

carrera f.   *race/career*
Me gustan las carreras de coches.
I like car races.

carretera f.   *highway*
Tomemos la carretera panorámica.
Let's take the scenic highway.

carro (rentado) m.   *(rental) car*
Un carro rentado es más económico que pagar taxis.
A rental car is cheaper than paying for taxis.

carta(s) f.   *letter, menu, playing cards*
Mesero, ¿me permite la carta?
Waiter, may I have the menu?

cartel m.   *poster*
Quiero comprar el cartel de la exposición.
I want to buy the poster of the exhibition.

cartelera f.   *show/movie listings*
Puedes encontrar la cartelera en el periódico.
You can find the movie listings in the newspaper.

cartera f.   *wallet*
Alguien me robó mi cartera.
Somebody stole my wallet.

cartero m.   *mailman*
El cartero reparte las cartas.
The mailman delivers the letters.

cartón m.   *cardboard*
Podemos enviar el regalo en una caja de cartón.
We can send the gift in a cardboard box.

casa (de campo, editorial) f.   *(country, publishing) house*
Elena trabaja en una casa editorial y tiene una casa de campo.
Elena works in a publishing house and has a country house.

casado/-a   *married*
Luisa y Jerónimo están casados.
Luisa and Jerónimo are married.

casarse   *to get married*
Se casaron el año pasado.
They got married last year.

cascada f.   *waterfall*
El Salto del Ángel es la cascada más alta del mundo.
Angel Falls is the world's tallest waterfall.

cáscara f.   *peel, shell*
Las nueces tienen una cáscara muy dura.
Walnuts have a very hard shell.

casco m.   *helmet*
Debes usar un casco en caso de haya un accidente.
You must wear a helmet in case there is an accident.

casi   *almost*
El tren casi siempre sale a tiempo.
The train almost always leaves on time.

caso m.   *case*
Es un caso legal difícil.
It is a difficult legal case.

castigar   *to punish*
Las leyes protegen a los inocentes y castigan a los criminales.
Laws protect the innocent and punish criminals.

castillo m.   *castle*
El castillo de Chapultepec en la Ciudad de México es muy bonito.
Chapultepec Castle in Mexico City is very pretty.

casualidad f.   *chance*
Llegamos aquí por casualidad.
We got here by chance.

catedral f.   *cathedral*
La catedral está en la plaza principal.
The cathedral is on the main square.

católico/-a   *Catholic*
La mayoría de las personas en Latinoamérica son católicas.
Most people in Latin America are Catholic.

causar   *to cause*
Los huracanes causan grandes daños en el Caribe.
Hurricanes cause great damage in the Caribbean.

cauteloso/-a   *cautious*
Seamos conductores cautelosos.
Let's be cautious drivers.

caza f. *hunting*
La caza era el deporte favorito de la realeza.
Hunting was royalty's favorite sport.

celebración f. *celebration*
El día de la independencia es una celebración nacional.
Independence Day is a national celebration.

celebrar *to celebrate*
Te invito a celebrar mi cumpleaños.
I invite you to celebrate my birthday.

celos m. pl. *jealousy*
Los celos pueden causar gran daño a una relación.
Jealousy can cause great damage to a relationship.

celoso/-a *jealous*
Mi esposo es muy celoso.
My husband is very jealous.

cementerio m. *cemetery*
Este cementerio es muy antiguo.
The cemetery is very old.

cenar *to eat dinner*
En España la gente cena muy tarde.
In Spain people eat dinner very late.

cenicero m. *ashtray*
No tengo ceniceros porque nadie fuma en la casa.
I don't have ashtrays because nobody smokes in the house.

ceniza f. *ash*
Las cenizas del volcán parecían copos de nieve.
The ashes from the volcano seemed like snowflakes.

centavo m. *cent (¢)*
El boleto cuesta diez pesos con cincuenta centavos.
The ticket costs ten pesos and fifty cents.

centro (comercial) m. *center, downtown/mall*
¿Quieres ir a pasear al centro o prefieres ir al centro comercial?
Do you want to go walk downtown or would you prefer going to the mall?

cepillo (de dientes) m.   *(tooth) brush*
Necesito comprar un cepillo de dientes.
I need to buy a toothbrush.

cerámica f.   *ceramics*
La cerámica artesanal es muy bonita pero muy cara.
Handcrafted ceramics are very pretty but very expensive.

cerca (de) f.   *fence/near*
Estamos cerca de la plaza principal.
We are near the main square.

cercano/-a   *close, near*
¿Dónde está el hospital más cercano?
Where is the nearest hospital?

ceremonia f.   *ceremony*
La ceremonia fue muy emotiva.
The ceremony was very moving.

cerrado/-a   *closed*
Los museos están cerrados los lunes.
Museums are closed on Mondays.

cerradura f.   *lock*
No tengo una llave para esta cerradura.
I don't have a key for this lock.

cerrar   *to close*
Por favor cierra la puerta cuando te vayas.
Please close the door when you leave.

cerrojo m.   *bolt*
Y cuando regreses no olvides echar el cerrojo.
And when you come back don't forget to slide the bolt.

certeza f.   *certainty*
No sé con certeza lo que sucedió.
I don't know with certainty what happened.

cesar   *to stop, to cease*
Los invitados no cesaron de bailar en toda la noche.
The guests didn't stop dancing all night long.

cesta f.   *basket*
La niña puso sus manzanas en la cesta.
The little girl put her apples in the basket.

champú m.   *shampoo*
Se me acabó el champú.
I ran out of shampoo.

charco m.   *puddle*
La lluvia dejó muchos charcos en el camino.
The rain left a lot of puddles on the road.

charlar   *to chat*
Charlemos por un rato.
Let's chat for a while.

checar   *to check*
Deberíamos checar el aceite del coche antes de salir.
We should check the motor oil before leaving.

cheque (de viajero) m.   *(traveler's) check*
Es más seguro viajar con cheques de viajero.
It is safer to travel with traveler's checks.

chico/-a   *adj. small/n. kid*
El chico de la casa de al lado tiene un coche chico.
The kid in the house next door has a small car.

chiflar   *to whistle*
Me gusta chiflar mientras trabajo.
I like to whistle while I work.

chismes m. pl.   *gossip*
Los chismes pueden arruinar la reputación de una persona.
Gossip can ruin a person's reputation.

chispa f.   *spark*
Una chispa puede provocar un incendio.
A spark can start a fire.

chiste m.   *joke*
Cuéntanos un buen chiste.
Tell us a good joke.

chistoso/-a   *funny*
Eres muy chistoso.
You are very funny.

chocar   *to collide, to crash*
Los coches chocaron en el cruce de caminos.
The cars crashed at the crossroads.

chofer m. & f. *chauffeur, driver*
El chofer del taxi fue muy amable.
The taxi driver was very nice.

choque m. *crash*
El choque detuvo completamente el tráfico.
The crash stopped traffic completely.

cibercafé m. *Internet café*
¿Sabes dónde puedo encontrar un cibercafé?
Do you know where I can find an Internet café?

ciego/-a *blind*
En España la lotería beneficia a los ciegos.
In Spain, the lottery benefits the blind.

cielo m. *sky*
¡Qué cielo tan azul!
What a blue sky!

ciencia (ficción) f. *science (fiction)*
Me gusta la ciencia y por eso me gustan las películas de ciencia
 ficción.
I like science and therefore I like science fiction movies.

cierto/-a *true, certain*
¡Eso no es cierto!
That is not true!

cigarrillo m. *cigarette*
¿Se pueden fumar cigarrillos aquí?
Can you smoke cigarettes here?

cine m. *cinema, movie theater*
¿Quieres ir al cine?
Do you want to go to the movies?

cinta f. *tape*
Necesito un pedazo de cinta adhesiva.
I need a piece of adhesive tape.

cinturón (de seguridad) m. *(seat) belt*
Es importante usar cinturones de seguridad.
It's important to wear seat belts.

circo m.   *circus*
Hay un circo en la ciudad.
There's a circus in the city.

cita f.   *appointment, date (social)*
Tengo una cita muy importante.
I have a very important appointment.

ciudad f.   *city*
La Ciudad de México es una ciudad enorme.
Mexico City is a huge city.

ciudadano/-a m./f.   *citizen*
Yo soy ciudadano de los Estados Unidos.
I am a United States citizen.

claro/-a   *clear, of course*
¿Quieres un café? ¡Claro!
Would you like a cup of coffee? Of course!

clase f.   *class*
Necesito ir a mi clase de español.
I have to go to my Spanish class.

clásico/-a   *classical*
Me gusta la música clásica.
I like classical music.

claxon m.   *car horn*
En algunas ciudades está prohibido tocar el claxon.
In some cities honking your car horn is forbidden.

cliente m. & f.   *client, customer*
Había muchos clientes en la tienda.
There were many customers in the store.

clima m.   *climate*
Cuernavaca tiene muy buen clima.
Cuernavaca has very good weather.

cloro m.   *bleach*
No use cloro para lavar mi ropa.
Don't use bleach to wash my clothes.

club (nocturno) m.   *(night) club*
¿Cuál es el mejor club nocturno por aquí?
What is the best nightclub around here?

cobarde   *coward*
No seas cobarde.
Do not be a coward.

cobija f.   *blanket*
Necesito otra cobija, por favor.
I need another blanket please.

cobrar   *to charge*
Cobran una cuota para entrar.
They charge a fee to get in.

coche (de alquiler) m.   *(rental) car*
Vine en un coche de alquiler.
I came in a rental car.

cocido m.   *cooked, stew*
Este cocido está muy sabroso.
This stew is very tasty.

cocina f.   *kitchen, cooking, cuisine*
Me encanta la cocina española.
I love Spanish cuisine.

cocinar   *to cook*
Sofía está cocinando la cena en la cocina.
Sofía is cooking dinner in the kitchen.

cocinero/-a m./f.   *cook*
Julio quiere ser cocinero porque le encanta la cocina.
Julio wants to be a cook because he loves cooking.

codicioso/-a   *greedy*
No seas codicioso.
Don't be greedy.

código (postal) m.   *(postal/zip) code*
Siempre debes escribir el código postal en el sobre.
You must always write the postal code on the envelope.

coger   *to grab, to take*
Coge un paraguas por si llueve.
Grab an umbrella in case it rains.

cojín m.   *cushion, pillow*
Necesito otro cojín para la cama.
I need another pillow for the bed.

cola f.   *line/tail*
Hice cola por dos horas para comprar los boletos.
I waited in line for two hours to buy the tickets.

colcha f.   *bedspread/comforter*
No tengo colcha para mi cama.
I do not have a bedspread for my bed.

colchón m.   *mattress*
El colchón es demasiado blando.
The mattress is too soft.

colección f.   *collection*
El museo está mostrando una interesante colección de pintura.
The museum is showing an interesting painting collection.

colega m. & f.   *colleague*
Tus colegas no son necesariamente tus amigos.
Your colleagues aren't necessarily your friends.

colegio m.   *(high) school*
¿Tienes que ir al colegio todos los días?
Do you have to go to school every day?

cólera m.   *cholera*
Los síntomas del cólera son vómito y diarrea.
Cholera symptoms are vomiting and diarrhea.

colgar   *to hang*
Puedes colgar tu ropa en el guardarropa.
You may hang your clothes in the closet.

colina f.   *hill*
El castillo está encima de la colina.
The castle is on top of the hill.

comedia f.   *comedy, play (Sp.)*
La comedia que vimos anoche no fue muy buena.
The play we saw last night wasn't very good.

comedor m.   *dining room*
¿Dónde está el comedor principal?
Where is the main dining room?

comentar   *to comment*
No comentaré sobre el asunto.
I will not comment on the matter.

comenzar   *to begin, to start*
El curso comienza el año próximo.
The course begins next year.

comer   *to eat, to have lunch*
Quiero algo de comer, por favor.
I would like something to eat, please.

comercio m.   *trade, commerce*
El tratado de libre comercio ha tenido resultados mixtos.
The free trade agreement has had mixed results.

cómico/-a   (as n.) *comedian*/(as adj.) *funny*
Me sucedió algo cómico hoy.
Something funny happened to me today.

comisaría f.   *police station*
Lo llevaron a la comisaría.
They took him to the police station.

como   *like, as*
Lo quiero como a un hermano.
I love him like a brother.

cómoda f.   (as n.) *chest of drawers*
Esta cómoda es una antigüedad valiosa.
This chest of drawers is a valuable antique.

cómodo/-a   (as adj.) *comfortable*
Me siento muy cómodo en tu casa.
I feel very comfortable in your house.

compañero/-a m./f.   *companion, mate*
Pedro es un buen compañero de viaje.
Peter is a good traveling companion.

compañía f.   *company*
Trabajo para una compañía pequeña.
I work for a small company.

compartir   *to share*
¿Podemos compartir la cuenta?
Can we share the bill?

complacido/-a   *pleased*
Estuve muy complacido con la conferencia.
I was very pleased with the conference.

completamente   *completely*
Yo también, completamente complacido.
I was also completely pleased.

complicado/-a   *complicated*
Es una situación complicada.
It's a complicated situation.

compra f.   *purchase*
Hice una buena compra en el mercado.
I made a good purchase at the market.

comprar(se)   *to buy*
¿Dónde puedo comprar artesanías?
Where can I buy handcrafts?

comprender   *to understand*
No te comprendo.
I do not understand you.

comprometerse   *to get engaged, to commit oneself*
Nos comprometimos a terminar el proyecto a tiempo.
We committed ourselves to finish the project on time.

compromiso m.   *commitment, engagement*
Tengo muchos compromisos esta semana.
I have many commitments this week.

computadora (portátil)   *computer, laptop*
Necesito una computadora para conectarme a la red.
I need a computer to connect to the Internet.

común   *common*
El arroz es muy común en la cocina hispánica.
Rice is very common in Hispanic cuisine.

comunicación f.   *communication*
La comunicación es la clave de una buena relación.
Communication is the key to a good relationship.

comunicar(se)   *to communicate*
Tratemos de comunicarnos en español.
Let's try to communicate in Spanish.

con (gusto)   *with (pleasure)*
¿Quieres ir al cine con Isabel y conmigo? ¡Con gusto!
Do you want to go to the movies with Isabel and me? With pleasure!

conciencia f.   *conscience*
Mi conciencia está en paz.
My conscience is at peace.

concierto m.   *concert*
El concierto de anoche fue maravilloso.
Last night's concert was wonderful.

concluir   *to conclude*
Para concluir la visita de la ciudad visitaremos la catedral.
To conclude the city tour we will visit the cathedral.

concurso m.   *contest/competition*
¿Quién ganó el concurso?
Who won the contest?

condición f.   *condition*
No podemos ir en estas condiciones.
We can't go under these conditions.

condimentado/-a   *seasoned, spicy*
No me gusta la comida muy condimentada.
I don't like very spicy food.

condón m.   *condom*
Es peligroso tener relaciones sexuales sin condón.
Having sex without a condom is dangerous.

conducir   *to drive, to conduct*
Conduce con cuidado.
Drive carefully.

conductor(a) m./f.   *driver*
Tomás es un buen conductor.
Tomás is a good driver.

conectar(se)   *to connect, to get connected*
¿Dónde puedo conectarme a la red?
Where can I connect to the Internet?

conexión (inalámbrica) f.   *(wireless) connection*
¿Hay una conexión inalámbrica en la habitación?
Is there a wireless connection in the room?

confesar(se)   *to confess*
Confieso que no lo sé.
I confess I don't know.

confiado/-a   *trusting/convinced*
No hay que ser demasiado confiado.
One shouldn't be too trusting.

confianza f.   *confidence, trust*
Te has ganado mi confianza.
You have gained my trust.

confirmar   *to confirm*
Debes de confirmar tu reservación antes de tu vuelo.
You must confirm your reservation before your flight.

confuso/-a   *confused*
Estoy perdido y confuso.
I am lost and confused.

congelado/-a   *frozen*
¿El pescado es fresco o congelado?
Is the fish fresh or frozen?

congestionado/-a   *congested*
La avenida está congestionada por la manifestación.
The avenue is congested because of the protest march.

conmigo   *with me*
¿Estás conmigo o en contra mía?
Are you with me or against me?

conocer   *to meet, to know*
Tengo mucho gusto en conocerte.
I am very pleased to meet you.

conocido/-a   *well-known*
Frida Kahlo es una conocida pintora mexicana.
Frida Kahlo is a well-known Mexican painter.

conocimiento m.   *knowledge*
No tengo muchos conocimientos de historia local.
I don't know a lot about local history.

consecuencia f.   *consequence*
Las acciones tienen consecuencias.
Actions have consequences.

conseguir   *to obtain / to achieve*
Consiguió una beca para estudiar en Perú.
He obtained a scholarship to study in Peru.

consejo m.   *advice*
Toma mi consejo.
Take my advice.

consentimiento m.   *consent*
Lo hicimos con su consentimiento.
We did it with his consent.

conserje m. & f.   *janitor/custodian/ receptionist/superintendent*
¿Sabe dónde está el conserje?
Do you know where the janitor is?

considerado/-a   *considerate*
Francisco es una persona muy considerada.
Francisco is a very considerate person.

construir   *to build*
Están construyendo un nuevo centro comercial en las afueras de
la ciudad.
They are building a new mall on the outskirts of the city.

consulado m.   *consulate*
Debo averiguar la dirección del consulado.
I must find out the consulate's address.

consultar   *to consult*
¿Necesitas consultar a un médico?
Do you need to consult a doctor?

contaminación f.   *pollution*
Debemos hacer algo para reducir la contaminación.
We must do something to reduce the pollution.

contaminado/-a   *contaminated, polluted*
Desgraciadamente, el lago está muy contaminado.
Unfortunately, the lake is very polluted.

contar   *to count, to tell*
Te voy a contar un cuento.
I am going to tell you a story.

contemporáneo/-a   *contemporary*
Quiero visitar el museo de arte contemporáneo.
I want to visit the contemporary art museum.

contener   *to contain/to hold*
Los bomberos pudieron contener el fuego.
The firemen were able to contain the fire.

contento/-a   *happy*
Estoy muy contento.
I am very happy.

contestar   *to answer, to reply*
Contesta el teléfono por favor.
Answer the telephone, please.

contigo   *with you*
Queremos ir contigo.
We want to go with you.

continuar   *to continue*
Continúa derecho para llegar al museo.
Keep going straight to get to the museum.

contra   *against*
Se tiene que hacer algo contra la adicción a las drogas.
Something must be done against drug addiction.

contrato (de arrendamiento) m.   *contract, lease*
Tengo que firmar el contrato de arrendamiento del apartamento.
I need to sign the apartment's lease.

conveniente   *convenient*
¿Cuál es un lugar conveniente para que nos encontremos?
Where's a convenient place to meet?

conversación f.   *conversation*
Tuvimos una agradable conversación.
We had a nice conversation.

copa f.   *(wine) glass*
Una copa de vino rojo, por favor.
A glass of red wine, please.

copia (de seguridad) f.   *copy, backup*
Este no es el original, es una copia.
This is not the original; it's a copy.

copiar   *to copy*
Siempre copio mis archivos por si acaso.
I always copy my files just in case.

corcho m.   *cork*
¿Me puedo quedar con el corcho de la botella de vino?
Can I keep the wine bottle's cork?

cordillera f.   *mountain range*
La cordillera de los Andes es impresionante.
The Andes mountain range is impressive.

correcto/-a   *right, correct*
Estás en lo correcto.
You're right.

corregir   *to correct*
Puede corregir mi español.
You may correct my Spanish.

correo (aéreo, electrónico) m.   *(air, e-) mail/post office*
¿Me puede decir dónde está el correo?
Can you tell me where the post office is?

correr   *to run*
Camina, no corras.
Walk, don't run.

corrupción f.   *corruption*
La corrupción es un problema en todas partes.
Corruption is a problem everywhere.

corrupto/-a   *corrupt*
Los oficiales corruptos abusan de su autoridad.
Corrupt officials abuse their authority.

cortauñas m.   *nail clippers*
¿Dónde puedo comprar un cortauñas?
Where can I buy a pair of nail clippers?

cortar(se)   *to cut*
Me corté el dedo cortando ajo.
I cut my finger while chopping garlic.

cortés   *polite*
En general, los mexicanos son muy corteses.
In general, Mexicans are very polite.

cortesía f.   *courtesy*
La cortesía es muy agradable.
Courtesy is very nice.

corto/-a *short*
Estos pantalones son demasiado cortos para mí.
These pants are too short for me.

cosa f. *thing*
¿Venden muchas cosas en el mercado de artesanía?
Do they sell many things at the handcraft market?

coser *to sew*
Necesito hilo para coser un hoyo en mi calcetín.
I need thread to sew mend a hole in my sock.

costa f. *coast*
Podemos ver la costa desde el barco.
We can see the coast from the ship.

costado m. *side*
Tengo un dolor en el costado.
I have a pain in my side.

costar *to cost*
¿Cuánto cuesta este cuadro?
How much is this painting?

costo m. *cost, price*
Su costo es incalculable.
Its price is invaluable.

costumbre f. *custom, habit*
La siesta es una costumbre popular en España.
Taking a nap after lunch is a popular custom in Spain.

costura f. *sewing, dressmaking, stitch*
Mi vestido necesita algunas costuras.
My dress needs some stitches to be mended.

costurera f. *seamstress*
Mi abuela era una costurera excelente.
My grandmother was an excellent seamstress.

cotidiano/-a *daily, everyday*
¿Cómo es la vida cotidiana en México?
What's daily life like in Mexico?

crear *to create*
Algunas personas crean—otras solamente copian.
Some people create—others just copy.

crecer   *to grow*
Las plantas crecen rápidamente en el trópico.
Plants grow quickly in the tropics.

(tarjeta de) crédito m.   *credit (card)*
¿Aceptan tarjetas de crédito?
Do they accept credit cards?

creer   *to believe*
Creo que el museo cierra a las cinco.
I believe the museum closes at five.

crema f.   *cream*
Necesito comprar crema humectante para mis manos.
I need to buy moisturizing cream for my hands.

cremallera f.   *zipper*
Prefiero los botones a las cremalleras.
I prefer buttons rather than zippers.

cremoso/-a   *creamy*
Tomamos un helado muy cremoso.
We had some very creamy ice cream.

crepúsculo m.   *dusk*
En el verano, el crepúsculo es alrededor de las siete.
During the summer, dusk is around seven.

crimen m.   *crime*
¿Hay mucho crimen en esa zona?
Is there a lot of crime in that area?

cristiano/-a   *Christian*
Soy cristiano pero no soy católico.
I'm Christian but not Catholic.

cruce (de caminos) m.   *crossroads*
En el cruce de caminos, den vuelta la derecha.
At the crossroads, turn right.

crucero m.   *cruise (ship)*
El crucero va de San Diego a Acapulco.
The cruise goes from San Diego to Acapulco.

cruda f.   *hangover*
Tengo una terrible cruda.
I have a terrible hangover.

crudo/-a *raw*
Es peligroso comer carne cruda.
It's dangerous to eat raw meat.

cruzar *to cross*
Crucemos la calle.
Let's cross the street.

cuaderno m. *notebook*
Voy a apuntar tu número de teléfono en mi cuaderno.
I am going to write your phone number in my notebook.

cuadra f. *city block*
De aquí al centro hay diez cuadras.
From here to downtown there are ten city blocks.

cuadro m. *picture, painting*
La galería tiene sobre todo cuadros de arte moderno.
The gallery has mainly modern-art paintings.

cualquier (cosa) *any (thing), whichever*
Podemos ir a verlas cualquier día.
We can go see them any day.

cualquiera *anyone*
No cualquiera puede pintar como Picasso.
Not anyone can paint like Picasso.

cuarentena f. *quarantine*
La epidemia obligó las autoridades a imponer la cuarentena.
The epidemic forced the authorities to impose a quarantine.

Cuaresma f. *Lent*
La Cuaresma viene después del carnaval.
Lent comes after the carnival.

cuarto m. *room*
¿Cuánto cuesta la noche en un cuarto doble?
How much is a double room per night?

cubeta f. *bucket*
Necesito una cubeta y un trapeador para trapear la cocina.
I need a bucket and a mop to mop the kitchen.

cubierta f.   *cover/ship's deck*
Hay mucha gente en la cubierta del barco despidiéndose con la mano.
There are many people on the deck waving good-bye.

cubiertos m. pl.   *silverware*
¿Me podría traer unos cubiertos limpios?
Could you bring me some clean silverware?

cubo m.   *cube, bucket*
El cubo se llenó con agua de lluvia.
The bucket filled up with rain water.

cubrir(se)   *to cover, to cover up*
Puedes cubrirte con esta cobija.
You can cover yourself with this blanket.

cuchara f.   *spoon*
La sopa se come con una cuchara.
You eat soup with a spoon.

cucharita f.   *teaspoon*
El café se mezcla con una cucharita.
You stir coffee with a teaspoon.

cucharón m.   *ladle*
La sopa se sirve con un cucharón.
Soup is served with a ladle.

cuchillo m.   *knife*
El cocinero necesita varios cuchillos.
The cook needs several knives.

cuenta f.   *account, bill (check)*
La cuenta, por favor.
The check, please.

cuento m.   *story*
¿Quieres que te cuente un cuento?
Do you want me to tell you a story?

cuerda f.   *rope*
Necesitamos una cuerda para colgar las hamacas.
We need a rope to hang the hammocks.

cuero m.   *leather*
Quiero comprar un cinturón de cuero.
I want to buy a leather belt.

cuesta f.   *slope*
Va a ser difícil subir la cuesta.
It is going to be difficult to climb the slope.

cueva f.   *cave*
Las cuevas de Altamira tienen pinturas prehistóricas.
The caves in Altamira have prehistoric paintings.

cuidado m.   *care, be careful!*
Tienes que tener cuidado.
You have to be careful.

cuidar(se)   *to take care, to look after*
¡Adiós! ¡Cuídate mucho!
Good-bye! Take good care of yourself!

culpa f.   *blame, guilt*
Nadie tiene la culpa.
No one is to blame.

culpable   *guilty*
Soy culpable.
I am guilty.

cumbre f.   *summit*
La cumbre de la montaña está sobre las nubes.
The mountain summit is above the clouds.

cumpleaños m.   *birthday*
¿Cuándo es tu cumpleaños?
When is your birthday?

cumplir (años)   *to accomplish, to turn (age)*
Mañana cumplo treinta años.
Tomorrow I turn thirty.

cuota f.   *fee/quota*
Tienes que pagar una cuota para entrar.
You have to pay a fee to get in.

cura f.   *cure*
Sería magnífico encontrar una cura para el cáncer.
It would be great to find a cure for cancer.

curiosidad f.   *curiosity*
La curiosidad mató al gato.
Curiosity killed the cat.

curioso/-a   *curious*
Era demasiado curioso.
He was too curious.

curso m.   *course, class*
Los cursos universitarios comienzan en septiembre.
University classes begin in September.

D

dama f.   *lady*
¡Bienvenidos, damas y caballeros!
Welcome, ladies and gentlemen!

dañar   *to harm*
No hay que dañar más el medio ambiente.
We mustn't harm the environment anymore.

dañino/-a   *harmful*
Fumar puede ser dañino a la salud.
Smoking can be harmful to one's health.

daño m.   *harm/damage*
El último huracán causó mucho daño.
The last hurricane caused great harm.

dar   *to give*
Silvia le dio un regalo de cumpleaños a Susana.
Silvia gave Susana a birthday present.

darse cuenta   *to realize*
No me di cuenta de que fuera tan tarde.
I didn't realize it was so late.

datos m. pl.   *data, information*
No tengo muchos datos sobre el asunto.
I don't have much information on the matter.

de   *from, of*
¿De dónde eres?
Where are you from?

debajo (de)   *under, beneath*
El gato está escondido debajo de la mesa.
The cat is hidden under the table.

deber   *must, to owe (money), duty*
Me debes cincuenta dólares y debes pagármelos.
You owe me fifty dollars and you must pay me.

débil   *weak*
Todavía me siento débil después de la enfermedad que tuve.
I still feel weak after the illness I had.

decepcionar   *to disappoint*
No te decepcionaré.
I will not disappoint you.

decidir(se)   *to decide*
No tienes que decidirte ahora mismo.
You don't have to decide right now.

decir   *to say, to tell*
Es difícil decir adiós.
It's hard to say good-bye.

decisión m.   *decision*
Debemos tomar una decisión ahora mismo.
We must make a decision right now.

declarar   *to declare, to state*
No tengo nada que declarar.
I don't have anything to declare.

dedicar(se)   *to devote (oneself), to work as*
Andrés se dedica a la carpintería.
Andrés works as a carpenter.

defectuoso/-a   *defective*
Esta computadora portátil está defectuosa.
This laptop is defective.

defender(se)   *to defend*
Traté de defenderme lo mejor que pude.
I tried to defend myself as best I could.

deforestación f.   *deforestation*
Debemos detener la deforestación.
We must stop deforestation.

dejar   *to leave, to allow, to set down*
¿Puedo dejar esto aquí?
Can I leave this here?

delatar   *to denounce, to expose*
La evidencia delató al criminal.
The evidence exposed the criminal.

delante (de)   *in front of*
El palacio municipal está delante de la iglesia.
The city hall is in front of the church.

delgado/-a   *thin*
Los españoles se mantienen delgados porque caminan mucho.
Spaniards keep thin because they walk a lot.

delicado/-a   *delicate*
Es una situación muy delicada.
It's a very delicate situation.

delicioso/-a   *delicious*
Este platillo está delicioso.
This dish is delicious.

demasiado/-a   *too much*
No me gusta beber demasiado.
I don't like to drink too much.

democracia f.   *democracy*
Creo que es preferible vivir en una democracia.
I think living in a democracy is preferable.

demora f.   *delay*
La demora del vuelo es de dos horas.
The flight's delay is two hours.

dentífrico m.   *toothpaste (Sp.)*
¿Dónde puedo conseguir dentífrico?
Where can I get toothpaste?

dentro (de)   *inside*
Todos están dentro de la casa porque hace frío afuera.
Everyone is inside because it's cold outside.

departamento m.   *department, apartment (L. Am.)*
Estoy buscando un departamento que no sea muy caro.
I am looking for an apartment which is not too expensive.

dependiente m. & f.   *clerk*
Pídele ayuda al dependiente de la tienda.
Ask the store clerk for help.

depositar   *to deposit*
Quisiera depositar este dinero en el banco.
I would like to deposit this money in the bank.

deprisa   *quickly*
Hay que terminar deprisa.
We must finish quickly.

derecha f.   *right (direction)*
Da vuelta a la derecha en la próxima esquina.
Turn to the right at the next corner.

derecho   *straight (ahead)*
Si caminas derecho encontrarás la dirección que estás buscando.
If you walk straight ahead you will find the address you are looking for.

derechos (civiles) m. pl.   *(civil) rights*
Los derechos civiles necesitan defenderse constantemente.
Civil rights need to be defended constantly.

derretir(se)   *to melt*
El hielo se derrite rápidamente con este calor.
Ice melts quickly in this heat.

desafortunadamente   *unfortunately*
Desafortunadamente, no los puedo acompañar.
Unfortunately, I can't go with you.

desagradable   *unpleasant*
Este lugar tiene un olor desagradable.
This place has an unpleasant odor.

desaparecer   *to disappear*
Muchas especies están a punto de desaparecer del planeta.
Many species are about to disappear from the planet.

desarrollar   *to develop*
Necesitamos desarrollar nuevas tecnologías para prevenir el
     calentamiento global.
We need to develop new technologies to prevent global warming.

desastre m.   *disaster*
Han sido víctimas de un desastre natural.
They are victims of a natural disaster.

desayunar   *to eat breakfast*
Vamos a desayunar temprano en la mañana.
We will eat breakfast early in the morning.

descansar   *to rest*
Necesito descansar antes de continuar.
I need to rest before going on.

descanso (tomar un) m.   *rest, break (take a)*
Te recomiendo tomar un descanso por la tarde.
I recommend that you take a break in the afternoon.

descargar   *to download*
No te olvides de descargar tus mensajes en la computadora.
Don't forget to download your messages on your computer.

descendiente m. & f.   *descendant*
El rey de España es descendiente de los reyes de Francia.
The king of Spain is a descendant of the kings of France.

desconectar   *to disconnect, to unplug*
Desconecta la plancha antes de salir.
Unplug the iron before leaving.

desconocido/-a   *unknown*
No temas a lo desconocido.
Don't fear the unknown.

descontento/-a   *dissatisfied, unhappy*
Mi esposa está descontenta con la habitación del hotel.
My wife is unsatisfied with the hotel room.

descortés   *impolite, rude*
Por favor no sea descortés con los huéspedes.
Please do not be rude to the guests.

describir   *to describe*
Describa lo que quiere comprar.
Describe what you want to buy.

descubrir   *to discover, to uncover*
Cristóbal Colón descubrió América.
Christopher Columbus discovered America.

descuento m.   *discount*
Lo puedo comprar si me da un descuento.
I can buy it if you give me a discount.

descuidado/-a   *careless*
Tuvo un accidente porque fue descuidado.
He had an accident because he was careless.

desde   *since*
Este restaurant ha estado abierto desde 1952.
This restaurant has been open since 1952.

desdén m.   *contempt*
Siento desdén por las personas deshonestas.
I feel contempt towards dishonest people.

desear   *to desire, to wish, to want*
Deseo tener una casa en la playa.
I wish I had a house on the beach.

desempacar   *to unpack*
Quiero desempacar antes de salir a cenar.
I want to unpack before going out to dinner.

desempleado/-a   *unemployed*
Mi esposo está desempleado desde mayo.
My husband has been unemployed since May.

deseo m.   *wish, desire*
Pide un deseo cuando veas la primera estrella.
Make a wish when you see the first star.

desesperado/-a   *desperate*
Estaba desesperado por verte.
I was desperate to see you.

desgracia f.   *misfortune*
¡Qué desgracia!
What a misfortune!

desleal   *disloyal*
Es imperdonable ser desleal.
It's unforgivable to be disloyal.

desnudo/-a   *naked*
Está prohibido asolearse desnudo en esta playa.
It is forbidden to sunbathe naked on this beach.

desodorante m.   *deodorant*
¿Dónde puedo comprar desodorante?
Where can I buy deodorant?

despacio   *slowly*
Camine despacio para evitar caerse.
Walk slowly to avoid falling.

despedir(se)   *to fire, to say good-bye*
Me voy a despedir temprano porque me esperan en casa.
I will say good-bye early because they are expecting me at home.

despejado/-a   *clear*
El cielo está despejado hoy.
The sky is clear today.

desperdiciar   *to waste*
No desperdicies tu energía en cosas vanas.
Don't waste your energy on useless things.

despertador m.   *alarm clock*
No olvides tu despertador porque lo necesitas para llegar a
    tiempo.
Do not forget your alarm clock because you need it to be on time.

despertar(se)   *to wake up*
No se puede despertar a tiempo sin el despertador.
He can't wake up on time without the alarm clock.

después   *after*
Cenaremos después de ir al cine.
We will have dinner after going to the movies.

destino m.   *destination, destiny*
Espero que llegue bien, cualquiera que sea su destino.
I hope you arrive safely, wherever your destination may be.

destruir   *to destroy*
No debemos de destruir nuestro planeta.
We should not destroy our planet.

desviación f.   *detour/diversion/deviation*
Tuvimos que tomar una desviación debido a la obra en la
    carretera.
We had to take a detour because of the roadwork.

detalle m. *detail*
Es importante fijarse en los detalles.
It's important to pay attention to detail.

detener(se) *to hold, to stop*
Es muy difícil detener un caballo que corre a toda velocidad.
It's very hard to stop a horse that's running at full speed.

detrás (de) *behind*
La fuente está en el centro de la plaza.
The fountain is in the middle of the square.

deuda f. *debt*
Afortunadamente pude pagar mis deudas.
Fortunately I was able to pay my debts.

devolver *to give back*
Le vamos a devolver su dinero.
We will give you back your money.

día (feriado/de fiesta) m. *day, holiday*
El día de Navidad es un día feriado.
Christmas day is a holiday.

diablo m. *devil*
El diablo está en los detalles.
The devil is in the details.

diariamente *daily*
Debe tomar esta medicina diariamente.
He must take this medicine daily.

diario *daily, newspaper*
Lee el diario todos los días.
He reads the newspaper every day.

dibujar *to draw (artistic)*
Ella dibuja flores lindas.
She draws lovely flowers.

dibujo m. *drawing*
Es un dibujo muy valioso de un artista francés.
It is a very valuable drawing by a French artist.

diferencia f. *difference*
No veo ninguna diferencia entre estos dos modelos.
I don't see any difference between these two models.

diferente *different*
Le aseguro que son radicalmente diferentes.
I assure you they are radically different.

difícil *difficult*
El español no es un idioma difícil de aprender.
Spanish is not a difficult language to learn.

dinero m. *money*
Necesito cambiar dinero.
I need to exchange money/currency.

dios *god*
Los aztecas tenían muchos dioses.
The Aztecs had many gods.

dirección f. *address, direction*
¿Tiene una dirección electrónica?
Do you have an e-mail address?

directo/-a *direct*
Hay muy pocos vuelos directos a Buenos Aires.
There are very few direct flights to Buenos Aires.

dirigir(se) *to direct, to manage, to head towards*
Nos dirigimos hacia el mercado para comprar artesanías.
We headed towards the market to buy handcrafts.

disco (compacto) m. *record, CD*
Quiero este disco en formato de disco compacto.
I want to buy this record in CD format.

discreto/-a *discreet, tactful*
Las personas discretas no cuentan chismes.
Tactful people don't gossip.

discriminación f. *discrimination*
A pesar de la retórica, todavía hay mucha discriminación racial.
In spite of rhetoric, there is still a lot of racial discrimination.

discriminar *to discriminate*
Cuando discriminamos atentamos contra los derechos civiles.
When we discriminate we threaten civil rights.

disculpa f. *apology*
Le debo una disculpa por mi tardanza.
I owe you an apology for my tardiness.

disculpar(se)   *to excuse, to apologize*
Discúlpeme, por favor.
Excuse me, please.

discutir   *to discuss, to argue*
No se debe de levantar la voz al discutir.
One should not raise one's voice when arguing.

disfrutar   *to enjoy*
Disfruté mucho la película.
I really enjoyed the movie.

disparar   *to shoot*
¡Me rindo, no dispare!
I give up, don't shoot!

disparo m.   *shot*
Estoy seguro de que anoche oí un disparo.
I'm sure I heard a shot last night.

distancia f.   *distance*
¿Cuál es la distancia entre Madrid y Barcelona?
What's the distance between Madrid and Barcelona?

distinto/-a   *distinct, different*
Elena es muy distinta de su hermana Marta.
Elena is very different from her sister Marta.

diversión f.   *entertainment, attraction*
La ciudad ofrece muchas diversiones.
The city offers many attractions.

divertido/-a   *amusing, fun, entertaining*
El viaje ha sido muy divertido.
The trip has been a lot of fun.

divertir(se)   *to amuse, to entertain, to have fun*
Nos divertimos mucho anoche.
We had a lot of fun last night.

divisa f.   *foreign currency*
Necesito comprar divisas para mi viaje.
I need to buy foreign currency for my trip.

divorciarse   *to get divorced*
Hace un año que se divorciaron.
They got divorced a year ago.

doblar   *to fold, to turn*
Cuando llegue al final de la calle doble a la izquierda.
When you reach the end of the street turn left.

doble m.   *double*
Estoy dispuesto a pagar el doble y hasta el triple.
I'm willing to pay double and even triple.

docena f.   *dozen*
Es más barato por docena.
It's cheaper by the dozen.

documento m.   *document*
No olvides hacer una copia de seguridad de tus documentos.
Don't forget to make a backup copy of your documents.

doloroso/-a   *painful*
Por suerte, la caída no fue muy dolorosa.
Luckily, the fall wasn't very painful.

dormido/-a   *asleep*
El niño se quedó dormido en el pasto.
The child fell asleep on the grass.

dormir(se)   *to sleep, to fall asleep*
Ayer nos dormimos antes de las diez.
Yesterday we fell asleep before ten.

dormitorio m.   *bedroom*
La casa tiene dos dormitorios.
The house has two bedrooms.

droga f.   *drug*
Las drogas son ilegales en la mayoría de los países.
Drugs are illegal in most countries.

drogadicción f.   *drug addiction*
La drogadicción tiene consecuencias terribles.
Drug addiction has terrible consequences.

ducha f.   *shower*
Voy a tomar una ducha antes de salir.
I'm going to take a shower before leaving.

ducharse   *to take a shower*
Es muy necesario ducharse por la mañana.
It is very necessary to take a shower in the morning.

dudar   *to doubt, to hesitate*
Dudo que este sea el camino correcto.
I doubt that this is the right road.

dudoso/-a   *doubtful*
Es dudoso que podamos llegar por aquí.
It's doubtful that we can get there through here.

dueño/-a m./f.   *owner*
¿Quién es el dueño de esta casa?
Who is the owner of this house?

dulce   *sweet/candy*
Alicia es muy dulce y le gustan mucho los dulces.
Alicia is very sweet and likes candy very much.

durante   *during*
No se pueden usar teléfonos celulares durante el vuelo.
You can't use cell phones during the flight.

durar   *to last*
Esta vela es muy pequeña y no va a durar prendida.
This candle is very short and won't stay lit long.

duro/-a   *hard*
Este pedazo de pan está muy duro.
This piece of bread is very hard.

E

eco m.   *echo*
Hay un eco aquí adentro, ¿lo oyes?
There's an echo in here, can you hear it?

economía f.   *economy*
La economía siempre está al borde de la crisis.
The economy is always on the brink of crisis.

económico/-a   *cheap, economical*
Estoy buscando un alojamiento económico.
I'm looking for a cheap place to stay.

edad f.   *age*
Te ves muy joven para tu edad.
You look very young for your age.

edición (electrónica) f. *edition/desktop publishing*
Esta es una mejor edición del libro.
This is a better edition of the book.

edificio m. *building*
Los edificios coloniales son muy bellos.
Colonial-style buildings are very beautiful.

editorial f. *publisher*
Este libro es editado por una editorial bien conocida.
This book is edited by a well-known publisher.

educación f. *education, manners*
La educación se adquiere en la escuela y la buena educación en la
   casa.
Education is acquired at school and good manners at home.

educativo/-a *educational*
La tienda del museo vende materiales educativos.
The museum store sells educational materials.

efectivamente *indeed, really*
Efectivamente, estas ruinas son muy antiguas.
Indeed, these ruins are very ancient.

efectivo/-a *cash/effective*
Pagué con un cheque porque no tenía efectivo.
I paid with a check because I didn't have cash.

egoísta *selfish*
No seas egoísta, préstame tu coche.
Do not be selfish, lend me your car.

ejecutivo/-a *executive*
Claudio es el director ejecutivo de una compañía de exportación.
Claudio is the executive director of an export company.

ejemplo m. *example*
La catedral es un ejemplo de arquitectura barroca.
The cathedral is an example of baroque architecture.

ejercicio m. *exercise*
El ejercicio físico es indispensable para la buena salud.
Physical exercise is necessary for good health.

ejército m.   *army*
Costa Rica no tiene ejército.
Costa Rica doesn't have an army.

elecciones f. pl.   *elections*
Los resultados de las elecciones fueron cuestionados por los
medios internacionales.
The election results were questioned by the international media.

electricidad f.   *electricity*
Ya no podríamos sobrevivir sin electricidad.
We couldn't survive without electricity anymore.

elegante   *elegant, fancy*
Tengo ganas de ir a cenar a un lugar elegante.
I feel like going to a fancy place for dinner.

elegir   *to choose, to elect*
Es difícil elegir un destino sin información.
It is difficult to choose a destination without information.

elevado/-a   *high, raised*
Las ruinas de Machu Picchu están en una cima muy elevada.
The ruins of Machu Picchu are on a very high summit.

elevador m.   *elevator*
Si hay un terremoto, no tomes el elevador.
If there's an earthquake, don't take the elevator.

embajada f.   *embassy*
La embajada está cerca del hotel.
The embassy is near the hotel.

embarazada f.   *pregnant*
Creo que estoy embarazada. / Creo que está embarazada.
I think I'm pregnant. / I think she's pregnant.

embarazo m.   *pregnancy*
Edgar está muy feliz por el embarazo de su esposa.
Edgar is very happy about his wife's pregnancy.

embarcar(se)   *to board*
¿A qué hora debemos embarcar?
At what time should we board?

emborracharse   *to get drunk*
Bebieron tanto que se emborracharon.
They drank so much that they got drunk.

embotellamiento m.   *traffic jam*
Los embotellamientos son muy frecuentes en la ciudad.
Traffic jams are very frequent in the city.

emergencia f.   *emergency*
¡Esto es una emergencia!
This is an emergency!

emocionado/-a   *excited*
Está muy emocionado por ir a Chile.
He is very excited about going to Chile.

emocional   *emotional*
Este viaje ha estado lleno de experiencias emocionales fuertes.
This trip has been full of strong emotional experiences.

emocionante   *exciting*
Será un viaje muy emocionante.
It will be a very exciting trip.

emotivo/-a   *emotional*
Despedirse de su familia fue muy emotivo.
Saying good-bye to his family was very emotional.

empacar   *to pack*
Es necesario empacar con cuidado antes de salir de viaje.
It's necessary to pack carefully before leaving on a trip.

empezar   *to begin, to start*
¿A qué hora empieza el espectáculo?
At what time does the show start?

empinado/-a   *steep*
Las escaleras de las pirámides son muy empinadas.
The steps of the pyramids are very steep.

emplear   *to employ, to use*
Empleo mi computadora todos los días.
I use my computer every day.

empleo m.   *job, employment*
Jorge no ha podido encontrar empleo.
Jorge hasn't been able to find a job.

empresa f.   *business*
La empresa para la que trabajo es muy exitosa.
The business that I work for is very successful.

empujar   *to push*
¡No me empujes!
Don't push me!

en (seguida)   *in, on, at (once)*
El dependiente nos atendió en seguida.
The store clerk assisted us at once.

en vez de   *instead of*
Compraré esta camisa en vez de aquélla.
I will buy this shirt instead of that one.

enamorarse (de)   *to fall in love*
Raquel y Alfonso se enamoraron a primera vista.
Raquel and Alfonso fell in love at first sight.

encantador/-a   *charming/delightful*
Mi vecino es encantador.
My neighbor is charming.

encantar   *to really like, to love*
Me encantan los atardeceres cerca de la playa.
I really like sunset evenings by the beach.

encendedor   *(cigarette) lighter*
¿Tienes un encendedor?
Do you have a lighter?

encender   *to light, to turn on*
¿Puedo encender la luz?
May I turn on the light?

enchufe m.   *electrical outlet/plug*
Necesito un enchufe trifásico para enchufar mi computadora.
I need a grounded, three-pin outlet to plug in my computer.

encima (de)   *on top of*
Coloqué los libros encima de la mesa.
I put the books on top of the table.

encoger   *to shrink*
Encogieron mis camisas en la lavandería.
They shrunk my shirts at the laundry.

encontrar(se)   *to find, to meet*
Podemos encontrarnos en la estación del tren.
We can meet at the train station.

enfadado/-a   *angry*
Espero que no estés enfadado conmigo.
I hope you're not angry with me.

enfrente (de)   *facing, in front of*
La agencia de viajes está enfrente de la oficina de correos.
The travel agency is in front of the post office.

engañar   *to deceive*
Te juro que no te estoy engañando.
I swear that I'm not deceiving you.

enojado/-a   *angry*
Carlos está muy enojado porque perdió su cartera.
Carlos is very angry because he lost his wallet.

enojar(se)   *to annoy, to anger, to get angry*
Mi hermano se enoja fácilmente.
My brother gets angry easily.

enorme   *huge*
La catedral de la Ciudad de México es enorme.
Mexico City's cathedral is huge.

enseñar   *to teach, to show*
El conductor le enseñó su licencia de manejar al policía.
The driver showed the policeman his driver's license.

entender   *to understand*
No entiendo lo que estás diciendo.
I don't understand what you are saying.

entonces   *then*
Entonces, no hay nada que decir.
Then, there is nothing to say.

entrada f.   *entrance, ticket*
Tenemos entradas para ir al cine esta tarde.
We have tickets to go to the cinema this evening.

entrar   *to enter*
Podemos entrar por aquí.
We can enter through here.

entre   *among, between*
Podemos repartir las palomitas entre nosotros.
We can share the popcorn among ourselves.

entregar   *to deliver, to hand over*
Le entregué los documentos al gerente.
I delivered the documents to the manager.

entrenamiento m.   *training*
El instructor de buceo tiene mucho entrenamiento en primeros auxilios.
The scuba diving instructor has a lot of training in first aid.

entrevista f.   *interview*
No quiero llegar tarde a mi entrevista.
I don't want to be late for my interview.

entusiasmado/-a   *excited*
Estoy muy entusiasmado con mi viaje a Ecuador.
I'm very excited about my trip to Ecuador.

envase m.   *container*
Pongamos la comida en envases de plástico.
Let's put the food in plastic containers.

enviar   *to send*
Te enviaré un correo electrónico en cuanto pueda.
I will send you an e-mail as soon as I can.

envolver (para regalo)   *to (gift) wrap*
No se te olvide envolver los regalos.
Do not forget to wrap the gifts.

equilibrado/-a   *balanced/well-adjusted*
Es más fácil llevar una carga bien equilibrada.
A well-balanced load is easier to carry.

equipaje m.   *luggage*
Es mejor no llevar mucho equipaje.
It's better not to take a lot of luggage.

equipo m.   *team, equipment*
Para bucear se necesita mucho equipo.
You need a lot of equipment to scuba dive.

equivocado/-a   *wrong*
Me temo que les dieron la información equivocada.
I am afraid they gave you the wrong information.

equivocarse   *to make a mistake*
Se equivocaron de dirección.
They made a mistake on the address.

error m.   *error, mistake*
Claramente hicimos un error al venir aquí.
Clearly we made a mistake coming here.

esbelto/-a   *slim, svelte*
El novio de mi hermana es esbelto y alto.
My sister's boyfriend is slim and tall.

escalar   *to climb*
Se necesita mucho equipo para escalar una montaña.
You need a lot of equipment to climb a mountain.

escalera f.   *ladder, staircase*
En caso de emergencia use las escalaras.
In case of emergency, use the stairs.

escapar(se)   *to escape*
Todos los huéspedes lograron escapar del incendio.
All the guests managed to escape from the fire.

escasez f.   *shortage*
La sequía provocó una escasez de comida.
The drought caused a food shortage.

escenario m.   *stage*
Me gustaría sentarme cerca del escenario.
I would like to sit near the stage.

escoba f.   *broom*
Toma la escoba y ponte a barrer.
Take the broom and start sweeping.

escoger   *to choose, to select*
No sé qué vestido escoger para el teatro.
I don't know which dress to choose for the theater.

esconder(se)   *to hide*
Los piratas escondieron grandes tesoros en el Caribe.
Pirates hid great treasures in the Caribbean.

escribir   *to write*
Escríbeme seguido, por favor.
Write to me often, please.

escritor(a) m./f.   *writer*
Carlos Fuentes es un famoso escritor mexicano.
Carlos Fuentes is a famous Mexican writer.

escritorio m.   *desk, desktop*
Puse los documentos sobre el escritorio.
I put the documents on the desktop.

escuchar   *to listen*
Escuchar música clásica es uno de mis pasatiempos favoritos.
Listening to classical music is one of my favorite pastimes.

escuela f.   *school*
La escuela está cerrada los fines de semana.
The school is closed on weekends.

escultura f.   *sculpture*
¿Te gusta la escultura?
Do you like sculpture?

ese/esa/esos/esas   *that, those*
Sí, pero no esa.
Yes, but not that one.

esencial   *essential*
El chocolate es el ingrediente esencial del mole poblano.
Chocolate is mole poblano's essential ingredient.

esfuerzo m.   *effort*
El esfuerzo trae recompensas.
The effort brings rewards.

esmeralda f.   *emerald*
Las esmeraldas colombianas son las mejores.
Colombian emeralds are the best.

eso   *that*
¿Qué es eso?
What is that?

espacio m.   *space*
No hay suficiente espacio en mi maleta para todos los regalos.
There isn't enough space in my suitcase for all the presents.

espacioso/-a   *roomy, spacious*
Necesito una más espaciosa.
I need a more spacious one.

español   *Spanish*
Es útil saber español.
It's useful to know Spanish. Knowing Spanish is useful.

espantar(se)   *to frighten, to get scared*
¡Me espantaste!
You scared me!

espantoso/-a   *frightful, horrible*
La película estuvo espantosa.
The movie was horrible.

esparcir   *to spread, to scatter*
Mi tío esparce las semillas en su huerta.
My uncle scatters the seeds in his vegetable garden.

especial   *special*
Este ha sido un viaje muy especial para mí.
This has been a very special trip for me.

especialidad f.   *specialty*
Es médico y su especialidad es la pediatría.
He is a doctor and his specialty is pediatrics.

especialista   *specialist*
Quiero ver a un especialista.
I want to see a specialist.

especialmente   *especially*
Venimos especialmente a verlos.
We came especially to see you.

especie (en peligro de extinción) f.   *(endangered) species*
Muchas especies de animales y plantas están en peligro de
    extinción.
Many animal and plant species are endangered.

espectáculo m.   *show, spectacle*
El espectáculo estuvo muy entretenido.
The show was very entertaining.

espejo m.   *mirror*
Deberías verte en el espejo.
You should look at yourself in the mirror.

esperanza f.   *hope*
Nunca se debe de perder la esperanza.
One should never lose hope.

esperar   *to hope, to wait, to expect*
Te voy a esperar enfrente de la iglesia.
I will wait for you in front of the church.

espeso/-a   *thick*
Me gustan las sopas espesas.
I like thick soups.

espíritu m.   *spirit*
Nos guía el espíritu de la aventura.
The spirit of adventure guides us.

esponja f.   *sponge*
¿Dónde está la esponja para lavar los vasos?
Where is the sponge to wash the glasses?

esquina f.   *corner*
Te puedo esperar en la esquina de la calle.
I can wait for you at the street corner.

estación (de policía) f.   *(police) station*
La estación de policía está cerca de la estación del trenes.
The police station is near the train station.

estacionamiento m.   *parking lot*
Es más seguro estacionarse en un estacionamiento.
It's safer to park in a parking lot.

estacionar(se)   *to park*
Es difícil estacionarse en esta ciudad.
It is difficult to park in this city.

estadio m.   *stadium*
Esta ciudad tiene un estadio de fútbol enorme.
This city has a huge soccer stadium.

estado m.   *state, condition*
No puede viajar en ese estado.
He can't travel in that condition.

estafa f.   *swindle, scam*
Este negocio es una estafa.
This business is a scam.

estallar   *to explode*
Los fuegos artificiales estallaron con un gran ruido.
The fireworks exploded with a big bang.

estampilla f.   *postage stamp*
¿Cuántas estampillas necesita esta carta?
How many (postage) stamps does this letter need?

estar   *to be (location, state)*
Estoy cansado pero contento de estar aquí.
I am tired but happy to be here.

estatua f.   *statue*
En la plaza hay una estatua de Simón Bolívar.
On the square there's a statue of Simón Bolívar.

este/esta/estos/estas este m.   *this, these/east*
Este es el libro que yo estaba buscando. La España está al este de
la costa este de los Estados Unidos.
*This is the book I was looking for. Spain is east of the United States'
east coast.*

estornudar   *to sneeze*
Estornudar puede ser un signo de gripa.
Sneezing may be a sign of the flu.

estrecho/-a   *narrow*
Las camas en este hotel son muy estrechas.
The beds in this hotel are very narrow.

estrella f.   *star*
Las estrellas parecen más brillantes cerca del mar.
Stars seem brighter by the sea.

estudiante m. & f.   *student*
Soy estudiante de ingeniería.
I'm an engineering student.

estudiar   *to study*
Tengo que estudiar para mis exámenes.
I have to study for my exams.

estudio m.   *study*
Tu computadora está en mi estudio.
Your computer is in my study.

estufa f.   *stove*
¿Tiene estufa el departamento?
Does the apartment have a stove?

estúpido/-a   *stupid*
No seas estúpido.
Don't be stupid.

etiqueta f.   *tag*
El precio está en la etiqueta.
The price is on the tag.

evitar   *to avoid*
Es necesario evitar los riesgos innecesarios.
It's necessary to avoid unnecessary risks.

exactamente   *exactly*
Le dije exactamente lo que estaba pensando.
I told him exactly what I was thinking.

exactitud f.   *accuracy*
En ingeniería, la exactitud es un requisito.
In engineering, accuracy is a requirement.

examen (médico) m.   *exam, (medical) examination*
¿Cuando fue su último examen médico?
When was your last (medical) examination?

examinar   *to examine*
El doctor lo puede examinar mañana por la mañana.
The doctor can examine you tomorrow morning.

excelente   *excellent*
La cena estuvo verdaderamente excelente.
Dinner was truly excellent.

exceso (de equipaje) m.   *excess (baggage)*
Me temo que lleva exceso de equipaje.
I'm afraid you are carrying excess baggage.

excursión f.   *excursion*
Mañana iremos de excursión todo el día a Machu Picchu.
Tomorrow we will go on an all-day excursion to Machu Picchu.

excursionista m. & f.   *day tripper*
Los excursionistas llegaron cansados y hambrientos.
The day trippers arrived tired and hungry.

existir   *to exist*
No existen los fantasmas, ¿o sí?
Ghosts don't exist, or do they?

éxito m.   *success*
La excursión fue un éxito.
The excursion was a success.

exitoso/-a   *successful*
Joaquín es un abogado exitoso.
Joaquín is a successful lawyer.

experiencia f.   *experience*
No tengo mucha experiencia pero lo intentaré de todos modos.
I don't have much experience but I will try anyway.

explicación f.   *explanation*
Las explicaciones que nos dieron no están claras.
The explanations they gave us aren't clear.

explicar   *to explain*
¿Me lo puede explicar usted otra vez?
Can you explain it to me again?

explotar   *to exploit, to explode*
Es fácil explotar a los pobres y a los ignorantes.
It's easy to exploit the poor and the ignorant.

exportación   *export*
Las exportaciones son una importante fuente de riqueza para
   Colombia.
Exports are an important source of wealth for Colombia.

exposición   *exhibition*
Hay una exposición de Frida Kahlo en el Museo de Arte
   Moderno.
There's a Frida Kahlo exhibition at the Modern Art Museum.

expreso/-a   *express*
Hay un autobús expreso que sale cada dos horas.
There's an express bus that leaves every two hours.

exterior m.   *outside*
¿Cuál es la temperatura exterior?
What's the outside temperature?

extraer   *to extract*
Venezuela extrae mucho petróleo.
Venezuela extracts a lot of oil.

extrañar   *to miss*
Extraño a mis amigos y a mi familia.
I miss my friends and family.

extranjero/-a   *foreign(er)*
Los extranjeros prefieren hospedarse en hoteles céntricos.
Foreigners prefer to stay at centrally located hotels.

extraño/-a   *strange*
Anoche oí un ruido extraño.
Last night, I heard a strange noise.

extraviado/-a   *lost*
¿Estás extraviado?
Are you lost?

F

fábrica f.   *factory*
Las fábricas suelen estar en las afueras de las ciudades.
Factories are usually on the outskirts of cities.

fabricante m. & f.   *manufacturer*
Los fabricantes de artesanías ponen sus estantes en el mercado.
Handcraft manufacturers set up their stalls at the market.

fácil   *easy*
Afortunadamente, el problema fue muy fácil de resolver.
Fortunately, the problem was very easy to solve.

facilitar   *to facilitate, to provide*
Conozco a alguien que puede facilitarnos la entrada al
    espectáculo.
I know someone who can facilitate our entrance to the show.

factible   *feasible/possible*
Con el equipo adecuado, es factible escalar la montaña.
With the right gear, climbing the mountain is feasible.

factura f.   *invoice*
¿A quién debo enviarle la factura?
Who should I send the invoice to?

falsificación f.   *forgery*
Esa pintura es una falsificación sin valor.
That painting is a worthless forgery.

falta f.   *lack/mistake*
He cometido una falta imperdonable.
I have made an unforgivable mistake.

faltar   *to lack*
Nos falta energía para llegar a la cima.
We lack the energy to get to the summit.

familiar   *familiar*
Tu cara me parece familiar.
Your face seems familiar.

famoso/-a   *famous*
Frida Kahlo es una pintora mexicana muy famosa.
Frida Kahlo is a very famous Mexican painter.

fantasma m.   *ghost*
Dicen que en esta vieja casa hay un fantasma.
They say that there is a ghost in this old house.

farol m.   *street lamp*
La luz de los faroles no deja ver la luz de las estrellas.
The light from the street lamps blocks out the star light.

fascinante   *fascinating*
Este libro sobre arqueología maya es fascinante.
This book on Mayan archaeology is fascinating.

fatigado/-a   *tired*
Estoy fatigado de visitar museos todo el día.
I am tired from visiting museums all day.

favor m.   *favor*
Tengo que pedirte que me hagas un favor.
I need to ask you to do me a favor.

favorable *favorable*
Espero que el clima sea favorable para la excursión.
I hope the weather is favorable for the excursion.

favorito/-a *favorite*
¿Cuál es tu película favorita?
What's your favorite movie?

fe f. *faith*
La fe mueve montañas.
Faith moves mountains.

fecha f. *date*
¿Cuál es la fecha de hoy?
What's today's date?

felicidad f. *happiness*
Todos estamos en busca de la felicidad.
We are all in search of happiness.

felicitaciones f. pl. *congratulations*
Felicitaciones por el premio que ganaste.
Congratulations on the prize you won.

feliz *happy*
Estoy feliz de estar aquí contigo.
I am happy to be here with you.

feo/-a *ugly*
Algunos piensan que el arte moderno es feo.
Some people think modern art is ugly.

feria f. *fair*
En la feria de artesanías encontrarás algunos regalos únicos.
At the craft fair you will find some unique gifts.

ferrocarril m. *railroad*
Es una pena que no haya más ferrocarriles.
It's a pity that there aren't more railroads.

fiesta f. *party*
Esta tarde hay una fiesta para celebrar el cumpleaños de Rita.
There's a party this afternoon to celebrate Rita's birthday.

fijo/-a *fixed*
No se puede regatear un precio fijo.
You can't bargain a fixed price.

fin (de semana) m.   *(week) end*
¿Qué planes tienes para el fin de semana?
What are your plans for the weekend?

final(mente)   *end, final(ly)*
No pudimos quedarnos hasta el final de la película.
We couldn't stay until the end of the movie.

fingir   *to pretend*
Le gusta fingir que es una estrella de cine.
She likes to pretend she's a movie star.

fino/-a   *fine, high quality*
Este encaje hecho a mano es muy fino.
This handmade lace is very high quality.

firma f.   *signature*
Ponga su firma aquí, por favor.
Put your signature here, please.

firmar   *to sign*
Debe de firmar el contrato antes de mudarse al departamento.
You must sign the contract before moving into the apartment.

flaco/-a   *skinny*
Héctor es un muchacho alto y flaco.
Hector is a tall and skinny boy.

flash m.   *flash*
Está estrictamente prohibido tomar fotos con flash.
Taking pictures with a flash is strictly forbidden.

flor f.   *flower*
Las rosas son las flores que más me gustan.
Roses are the flowers I like best.

florero m.   *flower vase*
Este florero antiguo es muy valioso.
This antique flower vase is very valuable.

flotar   *to float*
Los barcos flotan en el mar.
Boats float on the sea.

foco (Ec, Méx, Per) m.   *light bulb*
Esta linterna necesita pilas y también un foco nuevo.
This flashlight needs batteries and a new light bulb as well.

folleto m.   *brochure*
No olvides traer un folleto de la agencia de viajes.
Do not forget to bring a brochure from the travel agency.

fondo m.   *bottom, background*
El tesoro estaba en el fondo del mar.
The treasure was at the bottom of the sea.

forma f.   *shape, form*
Es mejor llenar la forma de aduana en el avión.
It is better to fill out the customs form on the plane.

fósforo m.   *match (light)*
Necesito un fósforo para prender esta vela.
I need a match to light this candle.

fotocopiadora f.   *photocopier/copying machine*
Necesito una fotocopiadora para copiar estas páginas.
I need a photocopier to copy these pages.

fotografía f.   *picture, photography*
Deja que te tome una fotografía.
Let me take your picture.

fracasar   *to fail*
Si lo intentamos seriamente, no fracasaremos.
If we try hard, we won't fail.

frágil   *fragile*
¡Cuidado! Este florero es muy frágil.
Careful! This flower vase is very fragile.

franco/-a   *frank, honest*
Un amigo franco es un amigo de verdad.
An honest friend is a true friend.

frasco m.   *jar*
Necesito frascos para poner la mermelada.
I need jars to store the marmalade.

frase f.   *sentence*
Las frases cortas son mejores.
Short sentences are better.

frazada f.   *blanket (L. Am.)*
Hace frío; necesito otra frazada.
It's cold; I need another blanket.

frecuente(mente) *frequent(ly)*
Es frecuente encontrar gangas en el mercado.
You can frequently find bargains at the market.

freír *to fry*
Mi hermana no sabe ni freír un huevo.
My sister doesn't even know how to fry an egg.

freno (de mano) m. *(hand) brake*
Necesitamos reparar los frenos del coche antes de seguir.
We need to repair the car's brakes before going on.

frente f. *front, forehead*
El frente de esta iglesia está en mal estado.
The front of this church is in bad shape.

fresco/-a *fresh, cool*
¿Están frescos estos huevos?
Are these eggs fresh?

frigorífico m. *refrigerator*
Veamos que podemos encontrar en el frigorífico.
Let's see what we can find in the refrigerator.

frío m. *cold*
Hoy hace mucho frío.
It's very cold today.

frontera *border*
Hay muchos problemas en la frontera entre México y los Estados Unidos.
There are many problems at the border between Mexico and the United States.

frotar *to rub*
Frótate las manos para calentarlas.
Rub your hands to warm them.

fuego m. *fire*
El fuego consumió el bosque.
Fire burned down the forest.

fuente f. *fountain, source, water spring*
El parque del Retiro tiene fuentes muy bellas.
The Retiro park has very beautiful fountains.

fuera (de)　　*out, outside*
¡Fuera de la casa!
Out of the house!

fuerte　　*strong, loud*
No puedo dormir porque la música está muy fuerte.
I can't sleep because the music is very loud.

fuerza f.　　*strength*
La unidad hace la fuerza.
There is strength in unity.

fumar　　*to smoke*
Ya no se permite fumar en la mayoría de las oficinas.
In most offices smoking is no longer allowed.

función　　*showing, performance*
¿A qué hora empieza la función?
At what time does the performance begin?

funcionar　　*to function*
Este radio sólo funciona con pilas.
This radio only functions with batteries.

futuro m.　　*future*
¿Qué planes tienes para el futuro?
What plans do you have for the future?

G

gafas f. pl.　　*eyeglasses*
No puede ver nada sin sus gafas.
He can't see a thing without his eyeglasses.

ganador(a) m./f.　　*winner*
¿Quién es ganador del concurso?
Who is the contest winner?

ganancia f.　　*profit, earnings*
La exportación genera muchas ganancias para el país.
Exports generate a lot of profits for the country.

ganar　　*to win, to earn, to gain*
Tomás ganó la carrera fácilmente.
Tomás won the race easily.

gancho m.   *hook, coat hanger*
Hay ganchos en el guardarropa.
There are hangers in the closet.

ganga f.   *bargain*
Se encuentran muchas gangas después de la época navideña.
You can find a lot of bargains after the Christmas season.

garantía f.   *guarantee*
Todos los aparatos electrónicos que compré tienen garantía.
All the electronics I bought have a guarantee.

gasolina f.   *gasoline*
En España la gasolina se vende por litro.
In Spain gasoline is sold by the liter.

gasolinera f.   *gas station*
Necesitamos encontrar una gasolinera pronto.
We need to find a gas station soon.

gastar   *to spend*
No podemos gastar el dinero en cualquier cosa.
We can't spend money on just anything.

gastos m. pl.   *expenses*
Algunos gastos son más importantes.
Some expenses are more important.

general(mente)   *general(ly)*
Generalmente, en México se come a las dos.
Generally, people eat at two in Mexico.

generoso/-a   *generous*
A veces los pobres son más generosos que los ricos.
Sometimes the poor are more generous than the rich.

gente f.   *people*
Este lugar está lleno de gente.
This place is full of people.

gerente m. & f.   *manager*
Necesito hablar con el gerente de la tienda.
I need to talk to the store manager.

gira f.   *tour*
Fuimos de gira por todo el país.
We went on a tour of the whole country.

gobierno m.   *government*
España todavía tiene un gobierno monárquico.
Spain still has a monarchic government.

golpe m.   *blow*
La mala noticia fue como un golpe doloroso.
The bad news was like a painful blow.

golpear   *to hit*
A veces la vida golpea muy fuerte.
Sometimes life hits hard.

gordo/-a   *fat, overweight*
No es sano estar gordo.
It's not healthy to be fat.

gota f.   *drop*
Gota a gota el agua se agota.
Water runs out drop by drop.

gotear   *to drip*
No pude dormir porque el grifo goteó toda la noche.
I couldn't sleep because the faucet dripped all night.

gozar   *to enjoy*
Mi abuelo ha podido gozar su retiro en buena salud.
My grandfather has been able to enjoy his retirement in good health.

grabación f.   *recording*
Quisiera comprar una grabación del concierto.
I would like to buy a recording of the concert.

gracias f. pl.   *thank you*
Gracias por su generosa ayuda.
Thank you for your generous help.

gracioso/-a   *graceful/funny*
Se necesita ser gracioso para bailar tango.
One needs to be graceful to dance the tango.

graduarse   *to graduate*
Ester se gradúa en la primavera.
Ester is graduating in the spring.

gramática f.   *grammar*
La gramática del español es muy regular.
Spanish grammar is very regular.

gran, grande   *big, large, great*
Su vecino tiene una casa grande pero un jardín pequeño.
His neighbor has a large house but a small garden.

granizo m.   *hail*
El granizo dañó el techo de la casa.
Hail damaged the roof of the house.

granja f.   *farm*
Me gustaría visitar una granja lechera.
I would like to visit a dairy farm.

granjero m.   *farmer*
Siempre quise ser un granjero.
I always wanted to be a farmer.

grano m.   *grain*
Los granos del maíz tienen un alto rendimiento.
Corn grains have a high yield.

grasa f.   *grease, fat*
Comer demasiada grasa no es sano.
Eating too much grease is not healthy.

gratis   *free (cost)*
Las mejores cosas en la vida son gratis.
The best things in life are free.

gratuito/-a   *free (cost), gratuitous*
Los jueves la entrada al museo es gratuita.
On Thursdays, entrance to the museum is free.

grave   *serious*
Espero que no sea nada grave.
I hope it's nothing serious.

grifo m.   *faucet*
El agua del grifo no es potable.
The water from the faucet is not drinkable.

gritar   *to shout, to scream*
No necesitas gritar.
You don't need to shout.

grosería f.   *rudeness, swear word*
Es de mala educación decir groserías.
Using swear words is bad manners.

grupo m.   *group*
Hay diez personas en nuestro grupo.
There are ten people in our group.

guapo/-a   *handsome*
Martín es un hombre muy guapo.
Martín is a very handsome man.

guardar   *to guard, to keep, to put away*
Deberías guardar el dinero en una caja de seguridad.
You should keep the money in a safe-deposit box.

guardia m.   *guard*
Siempre hay un guardia dentro del banco.
There is always a guard inside the bank.

guerra f.   *war*
Nadie gana en una guerra.
In a war, nobody wins.

guía (telefónica) f.   *guide, guidebook, phonebook*
Es más fácil viajar con una guía actualizada.
It's easier to travel with an updated guidebook.

guiar   *to guide*
¿Alguien nos puede guiar por el museo?
Can someone guide us through the museum?

guitarra f.   *guitar*
¿Sabes tocar la guitarra?
Can you play the guitar?

gustar   *to like*
Me gusta mucho la comida mexicana.
I like Mexican cooking a lot.

gusto m.   *taste, pleasure*
Mucho gusto en conocerlo.
It's a pleasure to meet you.

H

habilidad f.   *ability/skill*
Conozco algunos acordes, pero no tengo mucha habilidad.
I know some chords, but I don't have much skill.

habitación (doble) f.   *(double) room*
¿Tiene una habitación doble para dos noches?
Do you have a double room for two nights?

hablar   *to talk, to speak*
Quiero aprender a hablar español.
I want to learn how to speak Spanish.

hacer   *to do, to make*
¿Qué vas a hacer esta noche?
What are you doing tonight?

hacia   *toward*
Siga caminando hacia la estación de trenes y encontrará el hotel.
Continue walking toward the train station and you will find the hotel.

hacienda f.   *country estate*
Este hotel era una hacienda.
This hotel used to be a country estate.

hallar   *to find*
Tenemos que hallar el camino al hotel antes de que anochezca.
We have to find the way to the hotel before it gets dark.

hamaca f.   *hammock*
Una hamaca es lo mejor para una siesta.
A hammock is the best for a nap.

hambre f.   *hunger*
No tengo mucha hambre todavía.
I am not very hungry yet.

hasta   *until*
Te esperé hasta las ocho de la noche.
I waited for you until eight o'clock at night.

hay   *there is, there are*
Hay poco tiempo pero hay muchas cosas que hacer.
There is little time but there are a lot of things to do.

hecho/-a   *done, made*
Estas artesanías están hechas a mano.
These crafts are made by hand.

heladería f.   *ice-cream parlor*
Conozco una heladería donde hacen el mejor helado del mundo.
I know an ice-cream parlor where they make the world's best ice cream.

helar *to freeze*
Necesitamos más cobijas para no helarnos como anoche.
We need more blankets so we don't freeze like last night.

hermoso/-a *beautiful*
¡Qué lugar tan hermoso!
What a beautiful place!

héroe m. *hero*
Simón Bolívar es el héroe nacional de Venezuela.
Simón Bolívar is Venezuela's national hero.

herramienta f. *tool*
Guarda las herramientas cuando hayas terminado el trabajo.
Put away the tools when you have finished the job.

hervir *to boil*
Debes de hervir el agua del grifo antes de beberla.
You must boil the water from the faucet before drinking it.

hielo m. *ice*
Un vaso de agua sin hielo, por favor.
A glass of water without ice, please.

hierba f. *grass*
En Nicaragua cortan la hierba con machete.
In Nicaragua they cut the grass with machetes.

higiénico/-a *hygienic*
Este lugar no parece muy higiénico.
This place doesn't seem very hygienic.

hilo m. *thread*
No tengo suficiente hilo para cocer esta falda.
I do not have enough thread to sew this skirt.

hincha m. *sports fan*
Algunos hinchas llevan su fanatismo demasiado lejos.
Some fans take their fanaticism too far.

historia f. *history/story*
España es un país con mucha historia.
Spain is a country with a lot of history.

histórico/-a *historic*
El centro histórico está lleno de edificios de la época colonial.
The historic downtown district is full of buildings from the colonial period.

hogar m. *home*
Es agradable regresar al hogar después de un viaje largo.
It's nice to return home after a long trip.

hoja (de papel, de afeitar) f. *leaf, paper sheet, razor blade*
En el trópico los árboles nunca pierden las hojas.
In the tropics, trees never lose their leaves.

hola *hello*
Dile hola a tu hermano de mi parte.
Say hello to your brother on my behalf.

hombre m. *man*
Andrés es un hombre amable y generoso.
Andrés is a kind and generous man.

homosexual m. & f. *homosexual, gay*
El matrimonio entre homosexuales es legal en algunos países.
Marriage between homosexuals is legal in some countries.

hondo/-a *deep*
¿Qué tan honda es la piscina?
How deep is the pool?

honor m. *honor*
Antiguamente, las cuestiones de honor se resolvían con sangre.
In olden times, matters of honor were resolved with blood.

honradez f. *honesty*
La honradez es importante en la política.
In politics honesty is important.

honrado/-a *honest*
Los políticos deberían ser honrados.
Politicians should be honest.

horario m. *schedule*
¿Dónde puedo consultar el horario de los trenes?
Where can I check the train schedule?

hornear   *to bake*
Julia prometió hornear un pastel para mi cumpleaños.
Julia promised to bake a cake for my birthday.

horno m.   *oven*
En España, la temperatura del horno está en grados centígrados.
In Spain, oven temperature is in degrees centigrade.

horóscopo m.   *horoscope*
No creo en los horóscopos, pero me gusta leerlos.
I don't believe in horoscopes, but I like to read them.

huerta f.   *vegetable garden*
Estos tomates son de la huerta de mi tío.
These tomatoes are from my uncle's vegetable garden.

huésped m. & f.   *guest*
Usted es nuestro huésped de honor.
You are our honored guest.

huir   *to flee, to run away*
Los valientes no huyen ante el peligro.
The brave don't run away in the face of danger.

humedad f.   *humidity, dampness*
El calor y la humedad juntos son agotadores.
Heat and humidity together are exhausting.

húmedo/-a   *humid, damp*
No me gustan los lugares húmedos.
I don't like damp places.

humo m.   *smoke*
En un incendio, el humo puede ser tan peligroso como las llamas.
In a fire, smoke can be as dangerous as flames.

humor m.   *mood, humor*
Clara no tiene sentido del humor y siempre está de mal humor.
Clara doesn't have a sense of humor and she's always in a bad mood.

huracán m.   *hurricane*
En el Caribe los huracanes son muy frecuentes.
Hurricanes are frequent in the Caribbean.

I

idea f.   *idea*
Se me acaba de ocurrir una idea genial.
I just had a great idea.

identificación f.   *ID/ identification*
Se necesita identificación para poder entrar al club nocturno.
You need ID to get into the nightclub.

idioma m.   *language*
Me encanta aprender nuevos idiomas.
I really like learning new languages.

idiota m. & f.   *idiot*
¿Me tomas por un idiota?
Do you take me for an idiot?

iglesia f.   *church*
Esta iglesia data del siglo dieciséis.
This church dates from the sixteenth century.

igual(mente)   *same, likewise*
La comida mexicana en los EE.UU. no es igual a la comida en
  México.
Mexican food in the U.S. is not the same as food in Mexico.

igualdad f.   *equality*
La igualdad es un derecho humano fundamental.
Equality is a fundamental human right.

ilegal   *illegal*
Es ilegal y riesgoso importar semillas sin permiso.
It's illegal and risky to import seeds without a permit.

imaginar   *to imagine*
Imagínate las consecuencias.
Imagine the consequences.

impaciente   *impatient*
Es difícil no ponerte impaciente cuando estás de viaje.
It's difficult not to become impatient when you're traveling.

impedimento m.   *obstacle, impediment*
No veo ningún impedimento para nuestro viaje.
I do not see any obstacles for our trip.

importado/-a   *imported*
Hoy en día, la mayoría dela ropa es importada de China.
Today, most clothes are imported from China.

importante   *important*
Es importante hacer caso de las señales de tráfico.
It's important to pay attention to traffic signs.

imposible   *impossible*
Me temo que es imposible hacer lo que me pides.
I'm afraid that what you're asking me to do is impossible.

impresora (de tinta) f.   *(ink jet) printer*
Necesito una impresora para imprimir mi pase de abordar.
I need a printer to print my boarding pass.

imprevisto/-a   *unexpected*
Deben estar preparados para las situaciones imprevistas.
You should be prepared for unexpected situations.

impuesto m.   *tax*
En el aeropuerto venden productos libres de impuestos.
Duty-free products are sold at the airport.

incapaz   *incapable, unable*
Fuimos incapaces de alcanzar la cima de la montaña.
We were unable to reach the mountain summit.

incendio m.   *fire*
Debemos prevenir los incendios forestales.
We must prevent forest fires.

incierto/-a   *uncertain*
Los resultados de las elecciones son inciertos todavía.
The election results are still uncertain.

incluido/-a   *included*
Los impuestos ya están incluidos en el precio de la habitación.
Taxes are already included in the price of the room.

incluir   *to include*
No olvides incluir aspirinas en tu botiquín de primeros auxilios.
Don't forget to include aspirin in your first-aid kit.

incómodo/-a   *uncomfortable*
Viajar en avión puede ser muy incómodo.
Air travel can be very uncomfortable.

indeciso/-a   *undecided*
Perdió una buena oportunidad por ser indeciso.
He lost a good opportunity for being undecided.

indicar   *to indicate, to tell*
¿Puede indicarme cuál es el tren a Toledo?
Can you tell me which train goes to Toledo?

indigno/-a   *unworthy*
Me siento indigno de tantas atenciones.
I feel unworthy of so much attention.

indispensable   *necessary*
No es indispensable tener mucho dinero para viajar.
It isn't necessary to have a lot of money to travel.

industria f.   *industry*
La industria del café es muy importante en Colombia.
The coffee industry is very important in Colombia.

inexactitud   *inaccuracy*
La inexactitud en el horario puede causar confusión y retraso.
Inaccuracy in the schedule may cause confusion and delay.

infante m. & f.   *infant*
Los infantes pueden viajar en el regazo.
Infants may travel on your lap.

infeliz   *unhappy*
Tu partida me hace muy infeliz.
Your departure makes me very unhappy.

infiel   *unfaithful*
Ser infiel siempre trae malas consecuencias.
Being unfaithful always brings bad consequences.

influencia f.   *influence*
El dinero tiene mucha influencia en la política.
Money has a lot of influence in politics.

información f.   *information*
Necesitamos más información antes de tomar una decisión.
We need more information before making a decision.

informar   *to inform*
Nos acaban de informar que el vuelo está cancelado.
They just informed us that the flight is cancelled.

informática f.   *information technology*
César sabe mucho de informática.
César knows a lot about information technology.

ingeniero/-a m./f.   *engineer*
Mi primo Diego es ingeniero civil.
My cousin Diego is a civil engineer.

inglés m.   *English*
¿Hay alguien aquí que habla inglés?
Is there anyone here who speaks English?

ingrato/-a   *ungrateful*
No hay que ser ingrato.
One shouldn't be ungrateful.

ingredientes m. pl.   *ingredients*
Tenemos todos los ingredientes que indica la receta.
We have all the ingredients that the recipe calls for.

ingresos m. pl.   *income*
Este año la compañía espera recibir mayores ingresos.
The company expects to receive more income this year.

iniciar   *to begin, to initiate*
No inicies algo que no vas a terminar.
Don't begin something you won't finish.

injusto/-a   *unfair, unjustified*
La vida puede parecer injusta a veces.
Life can seem unfair sometimes.

inmediatamente   *immediately*
Si queremos llegar a tiempo debemos salir inmediatamente.
If we want to be on time we must leave immediately.

inmigración f.   *immigration*
La inmigración ilegal es en parte un resultado de la pobreza.
Illegal immigration is in part the result of poverty.

inmigrante m. & f.   *immigrant*
Los inmigrantes están buscando mejorar su calidad de vida.
Immigrants are looking to improve their quality of life.

inocente   *innocent*
Juro que soy inocente.
I swear I'm innocent.

inodoro f.   *toilet*
El inodoro está al fondo a la derecha.
The toilet is in the back to the right.

inquietud f.   *anxiety, restlessness*
Volar les provoca inquietud a algunas personas.
Flying causes anxiety in some people.

inquilino/-a m./f.   *tenant*
Los inquilinos de este edificio son ruidosos.
The tenants in this building are noisy.

insatisfecho/-a   *dissatisfied*
Estoy insatisfecho con el servicio en este hotel.
I'm dissatisfied with the service at this hotel.

inseguro/-a   *insecure, unsure, unsafe*
Este es un barrio inseguro por la noche.
This is an unsafe neighborhood at night.

insípido/-a   *bland*
No haya nada en la cocina española que sea insípido.
There is nothing bland in Spanish cuisine.

inspector(a) (de aduanas) m./f.   *inspector, customs officer*
Los inspectores de aduanas en la frontera son muy estrictos.
Customs officers at the border are very strict.

insulto m.   *insult*
Estos precios son un insulto y me rehúso a pagarlos.
These prices are an insult and I refuse to pay them.

inteligente   *intelligent*
Una persona inteligente sabe cuando cambiar de rumbo.
An intelligent person knows when to change course.

interconexión (de redes) f.   *network*
La interconexión de redes crece más y más rápido cada día.
The network grows bigger and faster every day.

interés m.   *interest*
Tengo poco interés por visitar museos.
I have little interest in visiting museums.

interesante   *interesting*
Ahora mismo hay exposiciones realmente interesantes.
Right now there are really interesting exhibitions.

intérprete m. & f. *interpreter*
Con este libro, no necesitamos un intérprete.
With this book, we don't need an interpreter.

interruptor m. *switch*
¿Dónde está el interruptor de luz del baño?
Where's the light switch for the bathroom?

inundación f. *flood*
Las inundaciones son comunes en la temporada de lluvias.
Floods are common during the rainy season.

inútil *useless*
Es inútil insistir.
It's useless to insist.

investigación f. *research*
Hice mucha investigación para preparar el viaje.
I did a lot of research in preparation for the trip.

investigar *to research*
Al investigar se aprenden muchas cosas.
Many things are learned by researching.

invitado/-a m./f. *guest*
Tenemos muchos invitados a cenar esta noche.
We have many guests coming for dinner tonight.

invitar *to invite*
¿Quieres invitar a alguien más?
Do you want to invite anyone else?

ir(se) *to go, to leave*
Es hora de ir a la fiesta, vámonos.
It's time to go to the party, let's go.

isla f. *island*
Algunas islas del Caribe eran guaridas de piratas.
Some islands in the Caribbean were pirate hideouts.

itinerario m. *itinerary*
La agencia de viajes me preparó un buen itinerario.
The travel agency prepared a good itinerary for me.

izquierda f. *left*
Si miran a la izquierda verán la Puerta del Sol.
If you look to the left you will see the Puerta del Sol.

J

jabón m.   *soap*
No hay jabón en el baño.
There is no soap in the bathroom.

jalar (L.Am.)   *to pull*
Es más fácil jalar las maletas que cargarlas.
It's easier to pull luggage than to carry it.

jamás   *never*
Jamás había visto algo así.
I had never seen anything like this.

jardín m.   *garden*
¿Te gustaría visitar el jardín botánico?
Would you like to visit the botanical garden?

jardinería f.   *gardening*
No me interesa la jardinería.
I'm not interested in gardening.

jardinero m.   *gardener*
Los jardineros cuidan celosamente los jardines del palacio.
The gardeners take care of the palace gardens zealously.

jarra f.   *pitcher*
Sirvieron jugo de fruta en lindas jarras de cristal.
They served fruit juice in lovely glass pitchers.

jarro m.   *jug*
Antiguamente se servía el vino en jarros de barro.
Wine was served in ceramic jugs in the old days.

jaula f.   *cage*
No soporto ver pájaros en jaulas.
I can't stand seeing birds in cages.

jefe/-a m./f.   *boss*
Claudia tiene suerte de tener un jefe tan bueno.
Claudia is lucky to have such a good boss.

joven m. & f.   *young*
Además es muy joven.
Besides, he's very young.

joya f. *jewel*
Las iglesias coloniales son verdaderas joyas arquitectónicas
Colonial churches are real architectural jewels.

jubilación f. *retirement*
Quiero aprovechar mi jubilación para viajar por el mundo.
I want to take advantage of my retirement to travel around the world.

juego m. *game*
Los juegos tradicionales están desapareciendo por los
videojuegos.
Traditional games are disappearing because of video games.

juez m. & f. *judge*
Un juez tiene que ser justo y objetivo.
A judge has to be fair and objective.

jugador(a) m./f. *player*
Algunos jugadores de futbol son casi héroes nacionales.
Some soccer players are almost national heroes.

jugar *to play (games, sports)*
¿Quieres jugar futbol en el parque?
Do you want to play soccer at the park?

juguete m. *toy*
Los juguetes hechos a mano son generalmente más bonitos.
Handmade toys are generally prettier.

juicioso/-a *sensible*
A veces es mejor ser juicioso que inteligente.
Sometimes it's better to be sensible than intelligent.

junta (directiva) f. *meeting/board of directors*
La junta directiva tuvo una junta con los trabajadores.
The board of directors had a meeting with the workers.

junto/-a(s) *next (to), together*
Queremos sentarnos todos juntos.
All of us want to sit together.

juramento m. *oath*
Un juramento es una gran responsabilidad.
An oath is a great responsibility.

jurar   *to swear*
Nunca jures en vano.
Never swear in vain.

justo   *fair*
¡Esto no es justo!
This isn't fair!

juventud f.   *youth*
Uno a veces no aprecia la juventud hasta que llega a viejo.
Sometimes one does not appreciate youth until one becomes old.

K

kilómetro m.   *kilometer*
Una milla equivale aproximadamente a tres kilómetros.
A mile is equivalent to approximately three kilometers.

L

lado m.   *side*
Me gusta caminar a tu lado.
I like to walk by your side.

ladrón(a) m./f.   *thief*
La policía atrapó al ladrón.
The police caught the thief.

lago m.   *lake*
Está prohibido pescar en el lago.
It's forbidden to fish in the lake.

lamentable   *regrettable*
Es lamentable que haya tanta pobreza en el mundo.
It's regrettable that there is so much poverty in the world.

lamer   *to lick*
Gracias al e-mail ya no tenemos que lamer las estampillas.
Thanks to e-mail we no longer have to lick postage stamps.

lámpara f.   *lamp*
La lámpara necesita un foco nuevo.
The lamp needs a new light bulb.

lana f.   *wool*
Aquí no se necesita un abrigo de lana.
Here you don't need a wool coat.

lapicero m.   *mechanical pencil*
Perdí mi lapicero.
I lost my mechanical pencil.

lápiz (labial) m.   *pencil, lipstick*
¿Me puedes prestar un lápiz?
Can you lend me a pencil?

largo/-a   *long*
Necesitas una cuerda más larga para escalar la montaña.
You need a longer rope to climb the mountain.

lástima f.   *pity*
El pobre emigrante me da lástima.
I feel pity for the poor emigrant.

lata   *(tin) can*
La sopa fresca es mejor que la sopa de lata.
Fresh soup is better than soup from a can.

lavabo m.   *bathroom sink*
Puedes lavarte las manos en el lavabo.
You can wash your hands in the bathroom sink.

lavadora f.   *washing machine*
¿Tiene lavadora el departamento?
Does the apartment have a washing machine?

lavar(se)   *to wash (oneself)*
Lavarse las manos antes de comer es importante.
It's important to wash one's hands before eating.

leal   *loyal*
Debe guardar un amigo leal como un tesoro.
One should treasure a loyal friend.

lección f.   *lesson*
El fracaso enseña una valiosa lección.
Failure teaches a valuable lesson.

lector(a) m./f.   *reader*
Un buen lector lee cada página.
A good reader reads every page.

leer   *to read*
A mí me encanta leer libros de viaje.
I really like reading travel books.

legal(mente)   *legal(ly)*
No se puede trabajar legalmente sin una visa de trabajo.
You can't work legally without a work visa.

lejano/-a   *distant*
Me gusta viajar a lugares lejanos.
I like to travel to distant places.

lejos (de)   *far (from)*
¿Qué tan lejos está Toledo de Madrid?
How far is Toledo from Madrid?

leña f.   *firewood*
Voy a buscar leña para hacer una fogata en la playa.
I'm going to look for firewood to make a bonfire on the beach.

lenguaje m.   *language*
Los animales tienen sus propios lenguajes.
Animals have their own languages.

lentamente   *slowly*
El tiempo parece pasar más lentamente cerca del mar.
Time seems to pass more slowly by the sea.

lentes m. pl.   *eyeglasses, lenses*
Mi madre necesita lentes para leer.
My mother needs eyeglasses to read.

lento/-a   *slow*
Un tren es más lento que un avión pero más cómodo.
A train is slower than a plane but more comfortable.

lesbiana f.   *lesbian*
Una de mis amigas es lesbiana.
One of my friends is a lesbian.

letra f.   *letter (alphabet)*
Las primeras letras del alfabeto son a, b y c.
The first letters of the alphabet are a, b, and c.

letrero m.   *(posted) sign*
El letrero indica por dónde ir.
The sign indicates which way to go.

levantar(se)   *to raise, to lift, to get up (out of bed)*
Levantarse temprano y levantar pesas levanta el ánimo.
Getting up early and lifting weights raises the spirit.

ley f.   *law*
Las leyes deben ser obedecidas.
Laws must be obeyed.

liberar   *to free, to liberate*
La verdad libera al hombre.
Truth frees man.

libra f.   *pound*
En España se mide el peso en kilos no en libras.
In Spain weight is measured in kilos not pounds.

libre (de impuestos)   *(duty) free, vacant*
¿Está libre este asiento?
Is this seat free?

libro m.   *book*
Un buen libro puede ser el mejor compañero de viaje.
A good book can be the best travel companion.

licencia (de conducir) f.   *(driver's) license*
Mi licencia de conducir caducó hace un mes.
My driver's license expired a month ago.

liga f.   *rubber band (L.Am.), league*
Muchos dominicanos juegan béisbol en las ligas mayores.
Many Dominicans play baseball in the major leagues.

ligeramente   *lightly*
Prefiero mi sopa ligeramente salada.
I prefer my soup lightly salted.

ligero/-a   *light(weight)*
En el verano se usa ropa ligera.
In the summer one wears light clothing.

lima (de uñas) f.   *(nail) file*
En general, los hombres no usan limas de uñas.
In general, men don't use nail files.

límite m.   *limit*
¿Cuál es el límite de velocidad en España?
What's the speed limit in Spain?

limpiar *to clean*
¿Puedo pasar a limpiar la habitación?
May I come in to clean the room?

limpio/-a *clean*
Mantener las manos limpias es muy importante.
It's very important to keep your hands clean.

lindo/-a *pretty*
Qué lindo vestido. ¿Cuánto cuesta?
What a pretty dress. How much is it?

línea f. *line*
Traté de llamarte pero la línea telefónica estaba ocupada.
I tried to call you but the telephone line was busy.

linterna f. *flashlight*
Préstame tu linterna para no perderme en la oscuridad.
Lend me your flashlight so I don't get lost in the dark.

liquidación f. *clearance sale*
Después de Navidad hay grandes liquidaciones.
After Christmas there are great clearance sales.

liso/-a *smooth*
Carla tiene el pelo muy liso.
Carla has very smooth hair.

lista f. *list*
La lista de invitados está muy larga
The guest list is very long.

listo/-a *clever/ready*
Porque es listo y estudioso ya está listo para ir a la universidad.
Because he's clever and studious he's ready to go to university.

literatura f. *literature*
¿Qué tipos de literatura te gusta leer?
What kinds of literature do you like reading?

llama f. *flame*
No te acerques demasiado a las llamas.
Don't get too close to the flames.

llamada f. *call*
Las llamadas de larga distancia pueden ser caras.
Long distance calls can be expensive.

llamar(se)   *to call, to be called*
Se llama María, llámala por teléfono.
Her name is María, call her on the phone.

llanta f.   *tire*
Necesitamos poner aire a las llantas.
We need to put air in the tires.

llave f.   *key*
Te daré una copia de la llave de la casa.
I'll give you a copy of the house key.

llegada f.   *arrival*
¿Cuál es nuestra hora estimada de llegada?
What's our estimated time of arrival?

llegar   *to arrive*
El vuelo llegó a tiempo.
The flight arrived on time.

llenar   *to fill*
Es mejor llenar las formas migratorias en el avión.
It's better to fill out the immigration forms on the airplane.

lleno/-a   *full*
El vuelo ya está lleno.
The flight is already full.

llevar   *to take, to carry*
¿Podemos pedir comida para llevar?
Can we get take-out food?

llorar   *to cry*
No llores, todo saldrá bien.
Don't cry; everything will turn out fine.

llover   *to rain*
¿Cree que va a llover?
Do you think it's going to rain?

llovizna f.   *drizzle*
La llovizna es una lluvia muy ligera.
Drizzle is a very light rain.

lluvia f.   *rain*
Me gusta bailar bajo la lluvia.
I like dancing in the rain.

lluvioso/-a   *rainy*
Leer ayuda a pasar el tiempo en un día lluvioso.
Reading helps pass the time on a rainy day.

localizar   *to locate*
Estoy tratando de localizar un buen hotel.
I'm trying to locate a good hotel.

loción f.   *lotion*
Usa una buena loción para conservar tu piel tersa.
Use a good lotion to keep your skin smooth.

loco/-a   *crazy*
¿Estás loco?
Are you crazy?

locura f.   *madness*
Hacer eso sería una locura.
Doing that would be madness.

lodo m.   *mud*
A los niños les encanta jugar con lodo.
Children love to play with mud.

lucha (libre) f.   *struggle, wrestling*
La lucha libre es muy popular en muchos países de
    Latinoamérica.
Wrestling is very popular in many Latin American countries.

luego   *later, afterward, then*
Luego de la siesta, podemos salir a pasear.
After our nap, we can go for a stroll.

lugar m.   *place*
¿Conoces un buen lugar para comer?
Do you know a good place to eat?

lujo m.   *luxury*
Viajar es un lujo necesario.
Traveling is a necessary luxury.

lujoso/-a   *lavish, luxurious*
Pero viajar lujosamente no lo es.
But traveling lavishly isn't.

luna (de miel) f.   *(honey)moon*
La luna de miel no duró mucho.
The honeymoon did not last long.

luz f.   *light*
La luz de la mañana es la mejor para tomar fotos.
The morning light is the best for taking pictures.

M

madera f.   *wood (material)*
Los juguetes de madera son más caros.
Wooden toys are more expensive.

madrugada f.   *the early hours (of the morning)/ very late at night*
Bailamos hasta la madrugada.
We danced until the early hours.

maduro/-a   *ripe*
No comas fruta que no está madura.
Do not eat fruit that isn't ripe.

maestro/-a m./f.   *teacher, master*
¿Cómo se llama tu maestro de español?
What's your Spanish teacher's name?

magia f.   *magic*
¿Crees en la magia?
Do you believe in magic?

mágico/-a   *magic(al)*
Esta es una noche mágica.
This is a magic night.

magnífico/-a   *magnificent*
Las pirámides de México son magníficas.
Mexico's pyramids are magnificent.

mago/-a m./f.   *magician*
Un buen mago nunca revela sus trucos.
A good magician never reveals his tricks.

mal   *bad(ly), ill*
¿Te sientes mal?
Do you feel ill?

maleta f.   *suitcase*
Mi maleta está llena de regalos para mi familia.
My suitcase is full of presents for my family.

maletín m.   *case (carrying)*
Llevo la computadora en su maletín.
I carry the computer in its carrying case.

malo/-a   *bad, evil*
Es malo ser una persona mala.
Being an evil person is bad.

malsano/-a   *unhealthy*
La contaminación crea un ambiente malsano.
Pollution creates an unhealthy environment.

mancha f.   *stain*
Una mancha de grasa no se quita fácilmente.
A grease stain can't be removed easily.

mandar   *to send, to order*
Te mandé un correo electrónico, ¿lo recibiste?
I sent you an e-mail, did you get it?

manejar   *to drive, to manage*
Es necesario manejar con cuidado.
It's necessary to drive carefully.

manera f.   *manner, way*
¿Cuál es la mejor manera de llegar al museo?
What's the best way to get to the museum?

manifestación f.   *demonstration, protest march*
El embotellamiento se debe a la manifestación.
The traffic jam is due to the protest march.

manso/-a   *tame*
Si vamos a andar a caballo quiero un caballo manso.
If we go horseback riding I want a tame horse.

manta f.   *blanket*
Si tienes frío, cúbrete con esta manta de lana.
If you're cold, cover up with this woolen blanket.

mantel m.   *tablecloth*
La mesa se ve mejor con mantel.
The table looks better with a tablecloth.

mantener   *to keep, to maintain*
Hay que mantener sano el medio ambiente.
We must keep the environment healthy.

mapa f.   *map*
Un buen mapa es imprescindible para el viajero precavido.
A good map is necessary for the cautious traveler.

maquillaje m.   *makeup*
Hay trucos de maquillaje para hacerte ver hermosa
There are makeup tricks to make you look beautiful.

máquina f.   *machine*
¿Cómo funciona esta máquina?
How does this machine work?

maquinaria f.   *machinery, mechanism*
¿Tiene una maquinaria complicada?
Does it have a complicated mechanism?

mar m.   *sea*
Me gustaría vivir cerca del mar.
I would like to live by the sea.

maravilla   *marvel*
Machu Picchu es una maravilla arquitectónica.
Machu Picchu is an architectural wonder.

maravilloso/-a   *wonderful*
Es un mundo tan maravilloso.
It's a wonderful world.

marca f.   *brand, marking*
A veces, la marca a solas vende el producto.
Sometimes, the brand alone sells the product.

marea (alta, baja) f.   *(high, low) tide*
Nadar en el mar cuando la marea está alta puede ser riesgoso.
Swimming in the sea when the tide is high can be risky.

mareado/-a   *seasick, dizzy*
Me siento mareado.
I feel dizzy.

mareo m.   *seasickness, dizziness*
¿Sufres de mareo?
Do you suffer from seasickness?

marinero m.   *sailor*
Los marineros deben saber nadar.
Sailors must know how to swim.

martillo m.   *hammer*
Venden martillos y clavos en la ferretería.
They sell hammers and nails at the hardware store.

más (que)   *more (than)*
La amistad vale más que el dinero.
Friendship is worth more than money.

más tarde   *later*
Nos vemos más tarde.
See you later.

masaje m.   *massage*
Un masaje me caería muy bien ahora mismo.
A massage would really make me feel good right now

matar   *to kill*
El torero mata al toro al final de la corrida.
The bullfighter kills the bull at the end of the bullfight.

matrimonio m.   *marriage*
En teoría, el matrimonio es para siempre.
In theory, marriage is forever.

mayor   *older, greater*
La gente mayor merece respeto.
Older people deserve respect.

mecánico m. & f.   *mechanic*
Necesitamos un mecánico que arregle nuestro coche.
We need a mechanic to fix our car.

mechero m.   *(cigarette) lighter*
Creo que dejé mi mechero en el restaurante anoche.
I think I left my lighter at the restaurant last night.

medida f.   *measure, measurement*
No es sano comer sin medida.
Eating without measure isn't healthy.

medio/-a   *half*
Tengo mucha hambre: me podría comer media docena de
    huevos.
I'm very hungry: I could eat a half-dozen eggs.

medios (de comunicación) m. pl.   *media*
Todos los medios de comunicación difundieron la terrible noticia.
All the media broadcast the terrible news.

medir   *to measure*
La calidad no siempre se puede medir por el precio.
Quality can't always be measured by price.

mejor   *better*
Es mejor viajar en temporada baja.
It's better to travel in the off-season.

mejorar(se)   *to improve, to get better*
Espero que pronto mejore tu situación.
I hope that your situation improves soon.

melodía f.   *tune*
Esa canción tiene una melodía que no me puedo sacar de la
    cabeza.
That song has a tune I can't get out of my head.

memoria f.   *memory*
Las fotografías son más confiables que la memoria.
Pictures are more trustworthy than memory.

mendigo m.   *beggar*
Suele haber mendigos afuera de las iglesias.
There are usually beggars outside churches.

menor   *younger, smaller*
Ernesto tiene un hermano menor y otro mayor.
Ernesto has one younger brother and one older.

menos (de, que)   *less (than)*
Quiero gastar menos de cien dólares en regalos.
I want to spend less than a hundred dollars on gifts.

mensaje (de texto) m.   *(text) message*
¿Recibiste mi mensaje?
Did you get my message?

menstruación f.   *menstruation*
La menstruación es un ciclo natural.
Menstruation is a natural cycle.

mente f.   *mind*
El aire fresco despeja la mente.
Fresh air clears the mind.

mentir   *to lie, to deceive*
¡No me mientas!
Don't lie to me!

mentira f.   *lie*
No hay mentiras pequeñas.
There are no small lies.

mentiroso/-a m./f.   *liar*
No hay que ser mentiroso.
One shouldn't be a liar.

menú m,   *menu*
¿Nos puede traer el menú por favor?
Can you bring us the menu please?

mercadeo m.   *marketing*
La publicidad es una herramienta del mercadeo.
Publicity is a marketing tool.

mercado (de valores) m.   *(stock) market*
¿Quieres ir al mercado de artesanías?
Do you want to go to the craft market?

mercancía f.   *merchandise*
La mercancía llegó dañada.
The merchandise arrived damaged.

mesa f.   *table*
Sentémonos a la mesa para cenar.
Let's sit at the table for dinner.

mesero/-a m./f.   *waiter*
El mesero sirvió la cena.
The waiter served dinner.

meseta f.   *plateau*
Gracias a su elevación, la meseta central tiene un clima templado.
Thanks to its elevation, the central plateau has mild weather.

mesita de noche f.   *nightstand*
Mi despertador está en la mesita de noche.
My alarm clock is on the nightstand.

metal m.   *metal*
El oro es caro por ser un metal raro.
Gold is expensive because it is a rare metal.

meter(se)   *to put in, to get in*
¿Podrás meter todo eso en tu maleta?
Will you be able to fit all that in your suitcase?

método m.   *method*
¿Cuál es el mejor método para empacar?
What's the best packing method?

metro m.   *subway*
Se puede llegar al aeropuerto en metro.
You can get to the airport on the subway.

mezcla   *mixture, blend*
La cocina mexicana tiene una mezcla de sabores particular.
Mexican cuisine has a particular blend of flavors.

mezclar   *to mix*
Mezclar los negocios con el placer puede ser riesgoso.
Mixing business and pleasure can be risky.

microondas m.   *microwave*
Nunca pongas metales en el microondas.
Never put metal in the microwave.

miedo m.   *fear*
Nunca hay que mostrar el miedo.
You must never show fear.

miedoso/-a   *fearful, cowardly*
Dicen que Gabriel es muy miedoso.
They say Gabriel is very cowardly.

mientras   *(mean)while*
¿Qué podemos hacer mientras esperamos?
What can we do while we wait?

milla f.　*mile*
Una milla equivale a tres kilómetros, más o menos.
One mile is the equivalent of three kilometers, more or less.

minusválido/-a　(adj. and noun) *handicapped*
¿Es accesible para los minusválidos este hotel?
Is this hotel accessible for the handicapped?

minuto m.　*minute*
Puedo estar listo en cinco minutos.
I can be ready in five minutes.

mirador m.　*lookout*
Desde el mirador la vista del valle es espectacular.
From the lookout the view of the valley is spectacular.

mirar　*to look (at)*
Es muy relajante mirar el mar.
Watching the sea is very relaxing.

misa f.　*Catholic mass*
No se puede visitar la iglesia durante la misa.
You cannot visit the church during mass.

mismo/-a　*same*
Nos quedamos en el mismo hotel que ustedes.
We stayed at the same hotel you did.

misterio m.　*mystery*
La decadencia de la civilización maya es un misterio.
The decadence of the Maya civilization is a mystery.

mitad f.　*half*
Si quieres, puedo pagar la mitad de la cuenta.
If you want, I can pay half of the bill.

mochila f.　*backpack, satchel*
Es más práctica una mochila que un portafolio.
A backpack is more practical than a briefcase.

moda f.　*fashion*
Buenos Aires es una de las capitales de la moda.
Buenos Aires is one of the capitals of fashion.

modelo m.　*model*
Quiero exactamente el mismo modelo pero en otro color.
I want exactly the same model but in a different color.

moderado/-a   *moderate*
Es más seguro conducir a una velocidad moderada.
It's safer to drive at a moderate speed.

módico/-a   *affordable/reasonable/moderate*
Busco un restaurante con precios módicos.
I am looking for a restaurant with affordable prices.

modo m.   *way, manner*
Le gusta hacer las cosas a su modo.
He likes to do things his way.

mojado/-a   *wet*
Ten cuidado: el piso está mojado.
Be careful: the floor is wet.

molestar   *to bother, to annoy*
Me molesta la gente grosera.
Rude people annoy me.

molestia f.   *bother, discomfort*
Los mosquitos son una molestia.
Mosquitoes are a bother.

momento m.   *moment*
¿Me puedes esperar un momento aquí?
Can you wait here for me a moment?

moneda f.   *coin, currency*
¿Cómo se llama la moneda peruana?
What's the Peruvian currency called?

montaña f.   *mountain*
El Aconcagua es la montaña más alta de las Américas.
Aconcagua is the tallest mountain in the Americas.

montañoso/-a   *mountainous*
La región montañosa ofrece hermosas vistas.
The mountainous region offers beautiful views.

montar (a caballo)   *to ride (on horseback)*
¿Podemos ir a montar a caballo?
Can we go horseback riding?

morder   *to bite*
No dejes que me muerda tu perro.
Don't let your dog bite me.

moreno/-a   *dark-haired/dark-skinned*
Las personas morenas son menos propensas a las quemaduras de
sol.
Dark-skinned people are less prone to sunburn.

morir   *to die*
¿Vale la pena morir por una idea?
Is it worth dying for an idea?

mosquitero m.   *mosquito net*
En muchas partes de Centroamérica no se puede dormir sin un
mosquitero.
*In many parts of Central America you can't sleep without a mosquito
net.*

mostrador m.   *counter*
Los clientes no pueden estar detrás del mostrador.
Customers can't be behind the counter.

mostrar   *to show*
¿Quiere que le muestre algo?
Would you like me to show you something?

mover(se)   *to move, to displace*
¡No te muevas!
Don't move!

muchacha f.   *young girl/maid*
Esa muchacha se llama Marta.
That girl's name is Marta.

muchacho m.   *young man*
Aquel muchacho es Miguel, su novio.
That young man over there is Miguel, her boyfriend.

muchas veces   *many times*
¿Has viajado muchas veces en tren?
Have you traveled on a train many times?

muchedumbre f.   *crowd*
La muchedumbre llenó el estadio.
The crowd filled the stadium.

mucho (gusto)   *much/(pleased to meet you)*
No nos queda mucho tiempo.
We don't have much time left.

mudo/-a m./f.   *mute*
Los mudos se pueden comunicar con las manos tan bien como
   cualquiera.
*Mutes can communicate with their hands as well as anybody can
   communicate.*

muebles m. pl.   *furniture*
Necesitamos muebles para el departamento.
We need furniture for the apartment.

muelle m.   *dock*
El barco llegó al muelle a tiempo.
The ship reached the dock on time.

muerte f.   *death*
No pensemos en la muerte.
Let's not think about death.

muerto/-a   *dead*
En México se celebra el Día de Muertos.
In Mexico, they celebrate the Day of the Dead.

muestra f.   *sample*
¿Le gustaría probar una muestra?
Would you like to try a sample?

mujer f.   *woman*
Eva fue la primera mujer según la Biblia.
Eve was the first woman according to the Bible.

multa f.   *fine, ticket*
Maneja despacio si no quieres recibir una multa.
Drive slowly if you don't want to get a ticket.

multitud f.   *crowd*
Había una multitud en la plaza.
There was a crowd in the town square.

mundo m.   *world*
El mundo es muy pequeño.
The world is very small.

muñeca f.   *doll*
Vi unas muñecas hechas a mano en el mercado.
I saw some handmade dolls at the market.

museo m.   *museum*
El museo de arte moderno es muy interesante.
The modern art museum is very interesting.

música f.   *music*
La música es un lenguaje universal.
Music is a universal language.

músico m. & f.   *musician*
Cuba tiene muchos grandes músicos.
Cuba has many great musicians.

muy (bien)   *very (well)*
Estoy muy bien, gracias.
I'm very well, thank you.

N

nacer   *to be born*
¿En qué día naciste?
On what day were you born?

nacional   *national*
El béisbol es el deporte nacional en la República Dominicana
Baseball is the national sport in the Dominican Republic.

nacionalidad f.   *nationality/citizenship*
Los puertorriqueños tienen nacionalidad estadounidense.
Puerto Ricans have U.S. citizenship.

nada   *nothing*
No hay nada que hacer.
There is nothing to do.

nadar   *to swim*
Nadar de noche en el mar es peligroso.
Swimming in the sea at night is dangerous.

nadie   *nobody*
Nadie aquí sabe inglés.
Nobody here knows English.

naipes m. pl.   *playing cards*
¿Quieres jugar a los naipes?
Do you want to play cards?

navaja (de afeitar) f.   *pocket knife/ (shaving) razor*
Pedro se cortó con la navaja de afeitar.
Pedro cut himself with the razor.

Navidad f.   *Christmas*
Te deseo una feliz Navidad.
I wish you a Merry Christmas.

necesario/-a   *necessary*
Es necesario tener una reservación.
It is necessary to have a reservation.

necesidad f.   *necessity/needs*
Todos tenemos las mismas necesidades.
We all have the same needs.

necesitar   *to need*
¿Necesitas ayuda?
Do you need help?

negar(se)   *to deny/to refuse*
Si lo sabes, no lo niegues.
If you know it, don't deny it.

negocio m.   *business, deal*
Jaime cerró el negocio con éxito.
Jaime closed the deal successfully.

neumático m.   *tire*
Se nos pincharon tres neumáticos en el camino.
We got three flat tires on the way.

ni   *nor*
Susana no quiso ni bailar ni cantar.
Susana did not want to sing nor dance.

niebla f.   *fog*
No se puede ver nada por la niebla.
You can't see a thing because of the fog.

nieve f.   *snow*
En el trópico sólo hay nieve en las montañas.
In the tropics there's only snow in the mountains.

ningún, ninguno/-a   *none*
Ninguno de nosotros sabe dónde estamos.
None of us knows where we are.

niño/-a m./f.   *child*
Este niño es hijo de Víctor.
This child is Víctor's son.

nivel m.   *level*
La Paz está a tres mil metros sobre el nivel del mar.
La Paz is nine thousand feet above sea level.

nombre m.   *name*
¿Cuál es tu nombre?
What's your name?

norte m.   *north*
Para evitar perderse hay que saber dónde está el norte.
To avoid getting lost you must know where north is.

notar   *to notice*
No noté la señal de desviación y me perdí.
I didn't notice the detour sign and I got lost.

novio/-a m./f.   *groom/bride, boy/girlfriend*
La novia y el novio se van a casar.
The bride and the groom are going to be married.

nube f.   *cloud*
Me preocupan esas nubes oscuras.
I'm worried about those dark clouds.

nublado/-a   *cloudy*
El cielo está nublado.
The sky is cloudy.

nuevamente   *again*
Intentemos nuevamente.
Let's try again.

nuevo/-a   *new*
Esta nueva edición es mejor que la anterior.
This new edition is better than the previous one.

nunca   *never*
Es mejor tarde que nunca.
It's better late than never.

O

o   *or, either*
¿Vienes o te quedas?
Are you coming or staying?

obedecer   *to obey*
A Juan no le gusta obedecer órdenes.
Juan does not like to obey orders.

objeto m.   *object*
Los objetos prehispánicos son muy valiosos.
Pre-hispanic objects are very valuable.

obligar   *to force*
Las circunstancias lo obligaron a hacerlo.
The circumstances forced him to do it.

obra f.   *work*
Esta pintura es una obra de arte.
This painting is a work of art.

obrero m. & f.   *worker*
Los obreros declararon una huelga general que paralizó al país.
The workers declared a general strike that paralyzed the country.

obtener   *to get, to obtain*
Tienes que trabajar duro para obtener lo que quieres.
You have to work hard to get what you want.

océano m.   *ocean*
El Canal de Panamá conecta el océano Atlántico con el Pacífico.
The Panama Canal connects the Atlantic Ocean with the Pacific.

ocupado/-a   *busy*
Joaquín siempre está ocupado.
Joaquín is always busy.

odiar   *to hate*
Odia su trabajo.
He hates his job.

oeste m.   *west*
Cristóbal Colón quería llegar a la India navegando hacia el oeste.
Christopher Columbus wanted to reach India by sailing west.

oficina f.   *office*
Tiene que ir a la oficina todos los días.
He has to go to the office every day.

oficio m.   *trade*
Manuel es un carpintero de oficio.
Manuel is a carpenter by trade.

ofrecer   *to offer*
¿Puedo ofrecerle algo de beber?
Can I offer you something to drink?

oído m.   *hearing/ear*
Roberto tiene mal oído.
Roberto has poor hearing.

oír   *to hear*
¿Oyes esa música?
Do you hear that music?

ola f.   *wave*
Las olas en el pacífico son mejores para surfear.
The waves in the Pacific are better for surfing.

oler   *to smell*
La comida huele bien.
The food smells good.

olla f.   *pot*
¿Qué se está cocinando en la olla?
What's cooking in the pot?

olor m.   *smell*
Aquí adentro hay un olor extraño.
There's a strange smell in here.

olvidar   *to forget*
No olvides la llave de casa.
Don't forget the house key.

operador(a) m./f.   *operator*
Necesito asistencia de la operadora para hacer esta llamada.
I need assistance from the operator to place this call.

opinión f.   *opinion*
No tengo opinión sobre el asunto.
I have no opinion on the matter.

oportunidad f.   *chance, opportunity*
Necesito otra oportunidad para probar que puedo hacerlo.
I need another chance to prove I can do it.

oración f.   *prayer/sentence*
Siempre estarás en mis oraciones.
You will always be in my prayers.

orden f.   *order, command*
Mesero, ¿puede tomarnos la orden?
Waiter, can you take our order?

ordenado/-a   *tidy/organized*
El cuarto está muy ordenado.
The room is very tidy.

ordenador m.   *computer (Sp.)*
Los ordenadores se han vuelto indispensables.
Computers have become indispensable.

ordenar   *to (put in) order, to command*
Estamos listos para ordenar la cena.
We are ready to order dinner.

organizar(se)   *to organize, to get organized*
Los obreros organizaron una gran manifestación.
The workers organized a big protest.

orgasmo m.   *orgasm*
El orgasmo no es necesariamente la mejor parte del sexo.
The orgasm is not necessarily the best part of sex.

orgullo m.   *pride*
Los fans de ese equipo tienen mucho orgullo.
That team's fans have a lot of pride.

orgulloso/-a   *proud*
Estoy muy orgulloso de mi hijo.
I'm very proud of my son.

original   *original*
Tu idea no es particularmente original.
Your idea is not particularly original.

orilla f.   *shore*
Ella vende conchas a la orilla del mar.
She sells seashells by the seashore.

oro m.   *gold*
No todo lo que brilla es oro.
Not all that glitters is gold.

orquesta f.   *orchestra*
La orquesta nacional dará un concierto para celebrar el día de la
independencia.
*The National Orchestra will give a concert to celebrate Independence
Day.*

oscuridad f.   *darkness*
¿Te asusta la oscuridad?
Are you afraid of the dark?

oscuro/-a   *dark*
En una noche oscura las estrellas brillan más.
The stars shine brighter on a dark night.

otra vez   *again*
Queremos pasar el día en la playa otra vez.
We want to spend the day at the beach again.

otro/-a   *another*
Necesito que me des otra oportunidad.
I need you to give me a second chance.

P

paciente   *patient* (as n., m.&f. *patient*)
Un buen viajero debe ser paciente.
A good traveler must be patient.

padecer   *to suffer*
Padecimos hambre y frío pero nos divertimos.
We suffered from cold and hunger but we had fun.

pagar   *to pay*
¿Puedo pagar con mi tarjeta de crédito?
Can I pay with my credit card?

página (electrónica) f.   *(web) page*
Tengo una página electrónica personal.
I have a personal web page.

pago m.   *payment*
El pago de la renta se debe hacer en el banco.
The rent payment must be made at the bank.

país m.   *country*
¿Cuántos países has visitado?
How many countries have you visited?

paisaje m.   *landscape, scenery*
¡Qué paisaje tan lindo!
What a beautiful landscape!

pala f.   *shovel*
Para hacer un buen castillo de arena se necesitan un cubo y una
    pala.
To make a good sand castle you need a pail and a shovel.

palabra f.   *word*
Estas son las palabras más útiles en español.
These are the most useful words in Spanish.

palacio m.   *palace*
Los reyes viven en el palacio real.
The King and Queen live in the Royal Palace.

palillo m.   *toothpick*
Creo que necesito un palillo.
I think I need a toothpick.

pañal m.   *diaper*
Los pañales de tela no son tan prácticos.
Cloth diapers are not very practical.

panorámico/-a   *panoramic, scenic*
La carretera panorámica a Acapulco es también más rápida.
The scenic highway to Acapulco is also faster.

pantalla f.   *screen*
La mayoría de las televisiones ahora tiene pantallas planas.
Most televisions now have flat screens.

pantalón (corto) m.   *trousers, shorts*
En verano usar pantalón corto es más cómodo.
Wearing shorts in summer is more comfortable.

pañuelo m.   *handkerchief*
Los pañuelos desechables son más prácticos.
Disposable handkerchiefs are more practical.

papel (higiénico) m.   *(toilet) paper*
Necesitamos comprar papel higiénico.
We need to buy toilet paper.

paquete m.   *package*
¿Dónde puedo enviar este paquete?
Where can I mail this package?

para   *for (recipient, purpose), to (direction/destination), in order to,*
     by (deadline)
El regalo para mi mamá estará listo para mañana.
The present for my mom will be ready by tomorrow.

parabrisas m.   *windshield*
Es más seguro conducir con un parabrisas limpio.
It's safer to drive with a clean windshield.

parada (de autobús) f.   *(bus) stop*
La parada de autobús está en la esquina de la calle.
The bus stop is at the corner of the street.

paraguas m.   *umbrella*
¿Crees que debamos llevar un paraguas?
Do you think we should take an umbrella?

parar(se)   *to stop, to stand up*
El autobús para en la esquina.
The bus stops at the corner.

parecer(se)   *to appear, to seem, to look like*
Parece que va a llover.
It looks like it's going to rain.

pared f.   *wall*
Dicen que las paredes tienen orejas.
They say that walls have ears.

pareja f.   *couple, partner*
Lorena y Rodrigo hacen buena pareja.
Lorena and Rodrigo make a good couple.

pariente m./f.   *relative*
Casi nunca visito a mis parientes.
I almost never visit my relatives.

parque m.   *park*
¿Quieres pasear por el parque después de comer?
Do you want to take a stroll in the park after eating?

parte f.   *part*
¿De qué parte de Chile eres?
What part of Chile are you from?

particular   *specific/private*
He tomado algunas lecciones particulares de español.
I have taken a few private Spanish lessons.

partido (político) m.   *match (sport), political party*
Vimos el partido de futbol en la televisión.
We watched the soccer match on T.V.

partir   *to depart/to split*
Ha llegado la hora de que partamos.
The time has come for us to depart.

pasado (mañana) m.   *past, (day after tomorrow)*
Salimos para Ecuador pasado mañana.
We leave for Ecuador the day after tomorrow.

pasaje m.   *passage, ticket*
El pasaje de avión fue muy caro.
The plane ticket was very expensive.

pasajero/-a m./f.   *passenger*
El pasajero perdió el avión.
The passenger missed the plane.

pasaporte m.   *passport*
Se necesita un pasaporte válido para viajar.
You need a valid passport to travel.

pasar   *to pass, to enter, to happen*
¿Qué pasó anoche?
What happened last night?

pasatiempo m.   *pastime*
El ajedrez es mi pasatiempo favorito.
Chess is my favorite pastime.

pase m.   *pass, permit*
Es muy conveniente poder imprimir los pases de abordar en casa.
It's very convenient to be able to print the boarding passes at home.

pasear   *to take a walk*
¿Quieres ir a pasear por el parque?
Do you want to take a walk in the park?

paseo m.   *walk, stroll, hike*
Tengo ganas de dar un paseo.
I feel like going for a stroll.

pasillo m.   *aisle*
Prefiero el asiento del pasillo a la ventanilla.
I prefer the aisle to the window seat.

pastilla f.   *pill, tablet*
Las pastillas para dormir pueden ser adictivas.
Sleeping pills can be addictive.

patear   *to kick*
El portero pateó la pelota al otro lado de la cancha.
The goalkeeper kicked the ball to the other side of the field.

patrón(a) m./f.   *employer, boss*
Mi patrón es una persona estricta pero simpática de todos modos.
My boss is a strict person but nice all the same.

paz f.   *peace*
Todos deseamos que haya paz en el mundo.
We all wish for peace on earth.

peatón m. & f.   *pedestrian*
En las ciudades grandes los peatones no tienen prioridad.
In big cities pedestrians don't have priority.

pedazo m.   *piece*
¿Me pasas un pedazo de pan?
Can you pass me a piece of bread?

pedido m.   *order, request*
Todavía no ha llegado su pedido.
Your order hasn't arrived yet.

pedir   *to ask for, to request*
Te tengo que pedir un favor.
I have to ask you for a favor.

pegar   *to hit, to glue*
Pégale duro a la piñata.
Hit the piñata hard.

peine m.   *comb*
¿Cuánto cuesta ese peine de carey?
How much is that tortoiseshell comb?

pelea f.   *fight*
No estoy buscando una pelea.
I'm not looking for a fight.

pelear   *to fight*
Los problemas no se resuelven peleando.
Problems aren't solved by fighting.

película f.   *movie, film*
¿Has visto esa película?
Have you seen that movie?

peligro m.   *danger*
Muchas especies están en peligro de extinción.
Many species are in danger of extinction.

peligroso/-a   *dangerous*
Manejar a alta velocidad es peligroso.
Driving at high speeds is dangerous.

pelota f.   *ball*
Aviéntame la pelota
Throw me the ball.

pena f.   *sorrow, shyness*
Pasa, no tengas pena.
Come in, don't be shy.

pensar   *to think*
¿En qué piensas?
What are you thinking about?

pensión f.   *boardinghouse*
Una pensión es más barata que un hotel.
A boardinghouse is cheaper than a hotel.

peor   *worse*
Hoy me siento peor que ayer.
Today I feel worse than yesterday.

pequeño/-a   *small, short*
Tomemos un pequeño descanso.
Let's take a short break.

perder(se)   *to lose, to miss (a flight), to get lost*
Es fácil perderse en esta ciudad.
It's easy to get lost in this city.

pérdida f.   *loss*
No podemos remediar la pérdida de su equipaje.
We can't remedy the loss of his luggage.

perdido/-a   *lost*
Creo que estamos perdidos.
I think we're lost.

perdonar   *to forgive, to excuse*
Es más fácil perdonar que olvidar.
It's easier to forgive than to forget.

perezoso/-a   *lazy*
No soy perezoso pero hoy estoy cansado.
I'm not lazy but today I'm tired.

perfecto/-a   *perfect*
Encontré el regalo perfecto en la feria de artesanías.
I found the perfect gift at the craft fair.

perfume m.   *perfume*
Ese perfume huele a una noche de primavera en un jardín.
That perfume smells like a spring night in a garden.

periódico m.   *newspaper*
Yo recibo el periódico todos los días.
I receive the newspaper every day.

permiso (de conducir) m.   *permission, driving permit*
No necesitas mi permiso para salir.
You don't need my permission to go out.

permitir   *to allow*
¿Se permite fumar aquí?
Is smoking allowed here?

pero   *but*
Fuimos al museo pero estaba cerrado.
We went to the museum but it was closed.

perseguir   *to pursue, to chase*
El perro me persiguió hasta la casa.
The dog chased me all the way home.

pertenecer   *to belong*
Esa bolsa no me pertenece.
That bag doesn't belong to me.

pesadilla f.   *nightmare*
Anoche tuve una pesadilla tan horrible que desperté gritando.
Last night I had such a horrible nightmare that I woke up screaming.

pesado/-a   *heavy*
El paquete está muy pesado.
The package is very heavy.

pesar   *to weigh*
¿Cuánto pesas?
How much do you weigh?

pescado m.   *fish*
¿Está fresco el pescado?
Is the fish fresh?

pescar   *to fish*
Lo pescaron esta mañana.
It was fished this morning.

pésimo/-a   *very bad, dreadful, terrible*
Pasé una noche pésima.
I had a very bad night.

peso m.   *weight*
¿Se vende por peso o por pieza?
Do you sell it by weight or by count?

picante   *spicy*
La comida mexicana es muy picante.
Mexican food is very spicy.

piedra f. *stone, rock*
Los mayas eran expertos en el tallado de la piedra.
The Maya were experts in stone carving.

piel f. *skin/leather, fur*
No necesitarás tu abrigo de piel en Cancún.
You won't need your fur coat in Cancún.

pila f. *battery*
¿Qué tipo de pilas necesita tu linterna?
What kind of batteries does your flashlight need?

píldora f. *pill*
¿Crees que necesitemos píldoras contra la malaria?
Do you think we need anti-malarial pills?

pinchar *to puncture*
¿Cómo se les pincharon las llantas?
How did your tires get punctured?

pintar *to paint*
Quisiera pintar un atardecer como este.
I would like to paint a sunset like this one.

pintor(a) m./f. *painter*
Goya es un famoso pintor español.
Goya is a famous Spanish painter.

pintura f. *painting*
Sus pinturas tienen un estilo muy particular.
His paintings have a very particular style.

pinzas f. pl. *tweezers*
Necesito unas pinzas para sacarme esta astilla.
I need tweezers to get this splinter out.

piscina f. *pool*
Vamos a tomar el sol cerca de la piscina.
Let's go sunbathe by the pool.

piso m. *floor, apartment (Sp.)*
¿Cuántos pisos tiene este edificio?
How many floors does this building have?

plancha f. *iron (for clothes)*
¿Tienes una plancha que prestarme?
Do you have an iron I can borrow?

planchar   *to iron*
Necesito planchar esta camisa para mi entrevista.
I need to iron this shirt for my interview.

plano/-a m.   *map/ (as adj., flat)*
Pedí un plano del museo.
I asked for a map of the museum.

planta (baja) f.   *plant/ (ground floor)*
Empecemos la visita por la planta baja.
Let's begin the visit on the ground floor.

plata f.   *silver*
Hay una exhibición de objetos de plata.
There's an exhibit of silver objects.

plato m.   *dish, plate*
Este es un plato de plata de la época colonial.
This is a silver plate from the colonial period.

playa f.   *beach*
¡Vamos a la playa!
Let's go to the beach!

plaza f.   *town square*
La multitud se reunió en la plaza.
The crowd gathered in the town square.

pluma f.   *feather/pen*
¿Puede prestarme su pluma?
Can I borrow your pen?

población f.   *population*
¿Cuál es la población de este pueblo?
What's this town's population?

pobre   *poor*
Aquí vive mucha gente pobre.
Many poor people live here.

pobreza f.   *poverty*
La pobreza es un grave problema.
Poverty is a serious problem.

poco/-a(s)   *little, few*
Existen pocas fuentes de trabajo.
Few sources of employment exist.

poder   *to be able to/* (as masculine noun) *power*
No hay nada que podemos hacer.
There is nothing we can do.

poderoso/-a   *powerful*
Los intereses económicos son muy poderosos.
Economic interests are very powerful.

podrido/-a   *rotten*
No comas esa fruta, está podrida.
Don't eat that fruit; it's rotten.

poesía f.   *poetry*
¿Te gusta la poesía?
Do you like poetry?

policía f./m. & f.   *police/police officer*
Hay que llamar a la policía.
We must call the police.

política f.   *politics*
La política tiene demasiados intereses en conflicto.
Politics has too many conflicting interests.

político/-a m./f.   *politician*
Los políticos nunca pueden darle gusto a todo el mundo al
    mismo tiempo.
Politicians can never please everybody at the same time.

poner(se)   *to put, to put on*
¿Dónde quieres que ponga esto?
Where do you want me to put this?

popular   *popular*
Los políticos populares saben hacer promesas.
Popular politicians know how to make promises.

por   *for, because of, around, by, through*
Vamos a hacer un viaje por barco por el Caribe.
We're going on a trip around the Caribbean by boat.

por eso   *therefore*
Me perdí, por eso llegué tarde.
I got lost, therefore I arrived late.

por favor   *please*
Tome asiento por favor.
Take a seat please.

por supuesto   *of course*
Por supuesto que me gusta viajar.
Of course I like to travel.

porción f.   *portion*
Sólo quiero una porción pequeña porque estoy a dieta.
I only want a small portion because I'm on a diet.

porque   *because*
Vamos porque se hace tarde.
Let's go because it's getting late.

portafolio m.   *briefcase*
No olvides tu portafolio.
Don't forget your briefcase.

portátil   *portable*
Mi portafolio es una oficina portátil.
My portfolio is a portable office.

poseer   *to possess*
Muchas personas no poseen suficientes recursos para vivir
    cómodamente.
Many people don't possess enough resources to live comfortably.

posible   *possible*
Creen que es posible mejorar su situación inmigrando.
They believe that it's possible to improve their situation by immigrating.

potable   *drinkable*
El agua de las fuentes no es potable.
Water from the fountains is not drinkable.

pozo m.   *(water) well*
Es como echar una moneda al pozo de los deseos.
It's like throwing a coin in the wishing well.

precio m.   *price*
Me parece que el precio está demasiado alto.
It seems to me that the price is too high.

predecir   *to predict*
Es imposible predecir el resultado de su apuesta.
It's impossible to predict the results of their wager.

preferir   *to prefer*
Algunos prefieren ir a la capital; otros al extranjero.
Some prefer to go to the capital; others abroad.

pregunta f.   *question*
Yo tengo una pregunta.
I have a question.

preguntar   *to ask*
No me preguntes por qué.
Don't ask me why.

premio m.   *prize*
El campeón de golf se ganó un premio.
The golf champion won a prize.

prenda f.   *garment*
Estas prendas son bonitas pero caras.
These garments are pretty but expensive.

preocupar(se)   *to worry*
No hay de qué preocuparse.
There's nothing to worry about.

preparar(se)   *to prepare, to get ready*
Lo mejor es prepararse para todo.
The best thing to do is to prepare for anything.

presentación f.   *presentation*
La presentación fue muy interesante.
The presentation was very interesting.

presentar(se)   *to present, to introduce*
Permítame que le presente a mi jefe.
Allow me to introduce you to my boss.

preservativo m.   *condom*
Los preservativos previenen las enfermedades venéreas.
Condoms prevent venereal diseases.

presión f.   *pressure*
Hay mucha presión para reducir el flujo de inmigrantes ilegales.
There is a lot of pressure to reduce the flow of illegal immigrants.

préstamo m.   *loan*
Los intereses del préstamo son demasiado altos.
The interest rates on the loan are too high.

prestar   *to lend*
¿Me puedes prestar dinero?
Can you lend me some money?

presupuesto m.   *budget*
No podemos gastar mucho porque tenemos un presupuesto
    limitado.
We can't spend a lot because our budget is limited.

prevenir   *to prevent*
Para prevenir las epidemias hay que mantener estrictas normas
    de higiene.
To prevent epidemics we have to keep strict hygiene regulations.

primer, primero/-a   *first*
Hoy es el primer día de nuestras vacaciones.
Today is the first day of our vacation.

principal   *main*
¿Cuál es la razón principal de su viaje?
What's the main reason for your trip?

principiar   *to begin, to start*
Lo más difícil es principiar una tarea.
The hardest thing is to begin a chore.

principio m.   *beginning*
Un buen principio no garantiza un buen fin.
A good beginning doesn't guarantee a good ending.

prisa f.   *hurry, rush*
Tengo prisa por llegar a la estación de tren.
I'm in a hurry to get to the train station.

prisionero/-a m./f.   *prisoner*
El drogadicto es un prisionero de su adicción.
The drug addict is a prisoner of his addiction.

privado/-a   *private*
Sería divertido tener un avión privado.
It would be fun to have a private plane.

probar(se)   *to prove, to taste, to try, to try on*
Quiero probar todos los platillos.
I want to try all the dishes.

problema m.   *problem*
La drogadicción es un problema social.
Drug addiction is a social problem.

procesador de palabras/de textos m.   *word processor*
Ya no puedo imaginar la vida sin los procesadores de palabras.
I can no longer imagine life without word processors.

producir   *to produce*
Las drogas se producen en el sur pero se consumen en el norte.
Drugs are produced in the south but they are consumed in the north.

profesión f.   *profession*
La profesión de la enseñanza paga poco pero tiene muchas
    recompensas.
The teaching profession pays little but has a lot of rewards.

profesor(a) m./f.   *teacher, professor*
Un profesor puede hacer una gran diferencia en la vida de un
    estudiante.
A professor can make a big difference in the life of a student.

profundo/-a   *deep*
La cueva más profunda de América está en México.
The deepest cave in the Americas is in Mexico.

programa (de computadora) m.   *program/computer software*
Ahora hay programas de computadora para todo.
Now there's computer software for everything.

prohibir   *to forbid*
El médico me prohibió fumar.
The doctor forbade me to smoke.

promesa f.   *promise*
No hagas una promesa que no estés dispuesto a cumplir.
Don't make a promise you're not willing to keep.

prometer   *to promise*
Prométeme que regresarás.
Promise me that you will return.

prometido/-a m./f.   *fiancé(e)*
Permítanme presentarles a Laura, mi prometida.
Allow me to introduce Laura, my fiancée.

pronosticar   *to forecast*
Han pronosticado un día espléndido para una excursión.
They have forecasted a splendid day for an excursion.

pronto   *soon, quickly*
Pronto estará lista la cena.
Dinner will be ready soon.

propiedad f.   *property*
¿De quién es esta propiedad?
Whose is this property?

propietario/-a m./f.   *owner*
El propietario es el señor Gómez.
The owner is Mr. Gómez.

propina f.   *tip*
La propina suele ser el quince por ciento.
The tip is usually fifteen percent.

propósito m.   *purpose*
El propósito de mi viaje es conocer España.
The purpose of my trip is to know Spain.

proteger   *to protect*
Hay que proteger el medio ambiente.
We must protect the environment.

protegido/-a   *protected*
Costa Rica tiene muchas zonas ecológicas protegidas.
Costa Rica has many protected ecological zones.

protesta f.   *protest*
La marcha de protesta duró todo el día.
The protest march lasted all day.

protestar   *to protest*
Los obreros protestaban por sus malas condiciones de trabajo.
The workers were protesting because of their poor working conditions.

próximo/-a   *next*
Nos bajamos en la próxima estación.
We're getting off at the next station.

prueba f.   *proof/test*
Tengo una prueba de español el viernes.
I have a Spanish test on Friday.

pudoroso/-a   *modest, chaste, virtuous*
Tania es muy pudorosa en el vestir.
Tania is very modest in her dress.

pueblo m.   *town, village/ people*
Este pueblo es muy pintoresco.
This town is very picturesque.

puente m.   *bridge*
Los incas construían largos puentes de cuerda.
The Incas built long rope bridges.

puerta (principal) f.   *(front) door, gate*
La puerta principal está cerrada.
The front door is closed.

pulsera f.   *bracelet*
¿Dónde compraste esa pulsera?
Where did you buy that bracelet?

puntual(mente)   *punctual(ly), on time*
Los trenes suelen ser más puntuales que los aviones.
Trains tend to be more punctual than planes.

puro/-a   (as adj.) *pure/*(as masculine noun) *cigar*
Los puros habanos valen como oro puro.
Havana cigars are worth as much as pure gold.

Q

quedar(se)   *to remain, to stay*
Es mejor quedarnos aquí hasta que pare de llover.
We had better stay here until it stops raining.

queja f.   *complaint*
¿Dónde puedo poner una queja?
Where can I lodge a complaint?

quejarse   *to complain*
No sirve de nada quejarse.
It's no use to complain.

quemado/-a   *burned*
Huele a quemado.
It smells like something burned.

quemar(se)   *to burn*
Usa crema solar para no quemarte.
Wear sunscreen so that you don't burn yourself.

querer   *to want, to love*
Raquel quiere mucho a Carlos.
Raquel loves Carlos very much.

querido/-a   *dear*
Gracias por venir, queridos amigos.
Thank you for coming, dear friends.

quincena f.   *fortnight (two weeks)/salary*
Recibo mi quincena cada quincena.
I get my salary every two weeks.

quitar(se)   *to remove, to get out of the way*
Ayúdame a quitar estas cosas de aquí.
Help get these things out of the way.

quizás   *maybe, perhaps*
Quizás llueva mañana.
Perhaps it will rain tomorrow.

R

rabino m.   *rabbi*
Los rabinos son los maestros de la tradición judía.
Rabbis are the teachers of the Jewish tradition.

radiador m.   *radiator*
Creo que el problema es una fuga en el radiador.
I believe the problem is a leak in the radiator.

rama f.   *branch*
El poder ejecutivo es una de las ramas del gobierno.
Executive power is one of the branches of government.

rápidamente   *rapidly*
Llegaremos más rápidamente en metro.
We'll get there more rapidly on the subway.

rápido   *fast*
Podemos ir a un lugar de comida rápida.
We can go to a fast-food place.

raro/-a   *weird, strange*
Este platillo es un poco extraño pero sabe delicioso.
This dish is a little strange but it tastes delicious.

razón f.   *reason*
No se necesita una buena razón para ser amable.
You don't need a good reason to be kind.

reacción f.   *reaction*
Espero que no te provoque una reacción alérgica.
I hope it doesn't cause you an allergic reaction.

real   *real/royal*
Realmente quiero visitar el palacio real.
I really want to visit the royal palace.

realista   *realistic*
Los patrones dicen que las demandas de los obreros no son realistas.
The employers say that the workers' demands aren't realistic.

rebaja f.   *discount*
Me hicieron un gran descuento en esta compra.
They gave me a great discount on this purchase.

rebanada f.   *slice*
¿Quieres una rebanada de pan con mantequilla?
Would you like a slice of bread with butter?

recargo m.   *surcharge*
Si no pagas puntualmente habrá recargos.
If you do not pay on time there will be surcharges.

recibir   *to receive*
¿Recibiste mi correo electrónico?
Did you receive my e-mail?

recibo m.   *receipt*
Cuando compres algo siempre pide un recibo.
When you buy something always ask for a receipt.

reciclar   *to recycle*
Reciclar es una manera de combatir el calentamiento global.
Recycling is a way to fight global warming.

reciente(mente)   *recent(ly)*
El conflicto entre patrones y obreros no es reciente.
The conflict between employers and workers isn't recent.

recomendar   *to recommend*
¿Me puedes recomendar un restaurante bueno pero barato?
Can you recommend a good but cheap restaurant?

reconocer   *to recognize*
No te reconocí.
I did not recognize you.

recordar   *to remember*
Recordaré este viaje por siempre.
I will remember this trip forever.

recorrido m.   *tour*
Quiero hacer un recorrido guiado por el museo.
I want to take a guided tour of the museum.

recto/-a   *straight (ahead)*
Si caminas recto llegarás a la plaza.
If you walk straight ahead you will get to the square.

recuerdo m.   *memory, souvenir*
Tengo agradables recuerdos de mi último viaje a Honduras.
I have nice memories of my last trip to Honduras.

redondo/-a   *round*
Es más barato un viaje redondo que uno sencillo.
A round-trip ticket is cheaper than a one-way one.

reducción f.   *reduction*
El boleto tiene una reducción del treinta por ciento para
    estudiantes.
The ticket has a thirty-percent discount for students.

reemplazar   *to replace*
Es hora de reemplazar estas pilas.
It's time to replace these batteries.

reflejar(se)   *to reflect, to be reflected*
Se dice que los ojos reflejan el alma de una persona.
It's said that the eyes reflect the soul of a person.

refrigerador m.   *refrigerator*
Las cervezas están en el refrigerador.
The beers are in the refrigerator.

refugiado/-a   *refugee*
Algunos inmigrantes son refugiados políticos.
Some immigrants are political refugees.

regalo m.   *gift*
Quiero comprar un regalo para mi madre.
I want to buy a gift for my mother.

regatear   *to bargain*
No me gusta regatear.
I do not like to bargain.

régimen m.   *regime/diet*
Los regímenes dictatoriales no pueden durar para siempre.
Dictatorial regimes can't last forever.

registrarse   *to check in, to register*
Después de registrarnos podemos ir a buscar algo de comer.
After checking in we can go find something to eat.

reglas f. pl.   *rules*
Si rompes las reglas tendrás que atenerte a las consecuencias.
If you break the rules, you'll have to live with the consequences.

regresar   *to return*
Regresaré a Europa algún día.
I will return to Europe some day.

rehusar   *to refuse*
Me rehúso a pagar los recargos.
I refuse to pay the surcharges.

reina f.   *queen*
La reina es la esposa del rey.
The queen is the king's wife.

reír(se)   *to laugh*
La mejor medicina es reírse.
The best medicine is to laugh.

relación f.   *relationship*
No es fácil mantener una relación de larga distancia.
Maintaining a long-distance relationship isn't easy.

relacionado/-a   *related*
Los problemas de la pobreza y la inmigración ilegal están
    relacionados.
The problems of poverty and illegal immigration are related.

religión f.   *religion*
La religión ha jugado un papel importante en la historia
    latinoamericana.
Religion has played an important role in Latin American history.

religioso/-a   *religious*
La primera orden religiosa que llegó a México fue la orden
    franciscana.
The first religious order to arrive in México was the Franciscan order.

reloj (de pulsera) m.   *clock, wrist watch*
Llegué tarde porque mi reloj está descompuesto.
I arrived late because my watch is broken.

remedio m.   *remedy, cure*
El amor es el mejor remedio.
Love is the best cure.

remitente m. & f.   *sender*
No olvides poner la información del remitente en el sobre.
Don't forget to put the sender's information on the envelope.

remplazar   *to replace*
Necesito remplazar las baterías de mi cámara.
I need to replace my camera's batteries.

rentar   *to rent, to lease*
¿Vas a rentar un departamento?
Are you going to rent an apartment?

reparación   *repair*
Este coche necesita una reparación urgente.
This car needs an urgent repair.

reparar   *to repair*
Necesitamos repararlo para seguir el viaje.
We need to repair it in order to go on with the trip.

repetir   *to repeat*
¿Puedes repetir lo que acabas de decir?
Can you repeat what you just said?

reproductor (de CD, MP3) m.   *(CD, MP3) player*
Los reproductores de MP3 se han vuelto muy populares.
MP3 players have become very popular.

resaca f.   *hangover (Sp.)*
Tengo una resaca terrible.
I have a terrible hangover.

reservación f.   *reservation*
La reservación está a nombre de la compañía.
The reservation is under the company's name.

reservar   *to reserve*
Hablé para reservar una mesa para cuatro ayer.
I called to reserve a table for four yesterday.

resistir   *to resist*
A veces es imposible resistir la tentación.
Sometimes temptation is impossible to resist.

resolver   *to solve*
Todo el mundo está tratando de resolver el problema del calen-
tamiento global.
Everybody is trying to solve the problem of global warming.

respetar   *to respect*
Podríamos empezar por respetar más a la naturaleza.
We could begin by respecting nature more.

respetuoso/-a   *respectful*
Jorge es una persona muy respetuosa.
Jorge is a very respectful person.

respiración f.   *breathing*
¿Sabes cómo dar respiración de boca a boca?
Do you know how to give mouth-to-mouth respiration?

respirar   *to breathe*
Es saludable respirar aire puro.
It is healthy to breathe fresh air.

responder   *to reply, to respond*
Trato de responder a los mensajes de texto tan pronto como los recibo.
I try to reply to text messages as soon as I receive them.

respuesta f.   *answer*
No tengo una buena respuesta a tu pregunta.
I don't have a good answer for your question.

restaurante m.   *restaurant*
Queremos ir a un restaurante de comida típica.
We want to go to a traditional-food restaurant.

retrasado/-a   *delayed*
El vuelo está retrasado a causa de la tormenta.
The flight is delayed because of the storm.

retraso m.   *delay*
No puedo justificar mi retraso.
I can't justify my delay.

retrato m.   *portrait*
Este es un retrato de Carlos Tercero (III).
This is a portrait of Carlos the Third.

reunión f.   *meeting*
Hoy tengo una reunión en mi oficina.
Today I have a meeting in my office.

reunir(se)   *to meet, to assemble*
Debemos reunirnos para discutir nuestro itinerario.
We must meet to discuss our itinerary.

revisar   *to review, to check*
Primero, tengo que revisar el mapa.
First, I have to check the map.

revista f.   *magazine*
Esta es una revista muy interesante.
This is a very interesting magazine.

revolver   *to stir*
La receta dice que hay que revolver constantemente sobre fuego lento.
The recipe says to stir constantly over low heat.

revuelto/-a *scrambled*
Me gustan los huevos revueltos.
I like scrambled eggs.

rey m. *king*
Carlos I era rey de España y de Alemania.
Carlos I was king of Spain and Germany.

rezar *to pray*
La gente reza en la iglesia.
People pray in church.

rico/-a *rich/tasty*
La comida mexicana es muy rica.
Mexican food is very tasty.

riesgo m. *risk*
A algunas personas les encanta tomar riesgos innecesarios.
Some people really like taking unnecessary risks.

riesgoso/-a *risky*
Muchas actividades son divertidas precisamente porque son
  riesgosas.
Many activities are fun precisely because they are risky.

río m. *river*
¿Podemos bañarnos en el río?
Can we bathe in the river?

riqueza f. *wealth*
La riqueza en este país es tan evidente como la pobreza.
Wealth in this country is as evident as poverty.

risa f. *laughter*
La risa es sana para el alma.
Laughter is healthy for the soul.

ritmo m. *rhythm*
Los ritmos africanos son el corazón de la música latina.
African rhythms are at the heart of Latin music.

robar *to steal*
Alguien me robó la cartera.
Somebody stole my wallet.

robo m.   *robbery, theft*
Hubo un robo en el banco.
There was a robbery at the bank.

roca f.   *rock, stone*
En Baja California el mar ha creado hermosas formaciones de
   roca.
The sea has created some beautiful rock formations in Baja California.

romántico/-a   *romantic*
El tango es un baile más sensual que romántico.
The tango is more a sensual than a romantic dance.

romper(se)   *to break*
Se cayó y se rompió la pierna.
She fell and broke her leg.

ropa (interior, de cama) f.   *clothes, underwear, bed linen*
No olvides empacar suficiente ropa interior.
Don't forget to pack enough underwear.

ropero m.   *closet, wardrobe*
La ropa de cama está en el ropero.
The bed linen is in the closet.

roto/-a   *broken*
Su pierna está rota.
Her leg is broken.

rubio/-a   *blond/e*
Juana tiene el pelo rubio.
Juana has blond hair.

rueda f.   *wheel*
Las maletas con ruedas son más prácticas.
Suitcases with wheels are more practical.

ruido m.   *noise*
¿Qué es ese ruido espantoso?
What's that frightful noise?

ruidoso/-a   *noisy*
Esta es una avenida muy ruidosa.
This is a very noisy avenue.

ruinas f. pl.   *ruins*
Las ruinas mayas son atracciones turísticas muy populares.
The Mayan ruins are very popular tourist attractions.

ruta f.   *route*
Las rutas poco conocidas son muchas veces las más interesantes.
Little-known routes are often the most interesting.

S

sábana f.   *sheet*
¿Quiere que cambie las sábanas?
Do you want me to change the sheets?

saber (a)   *to know, to taste like*
Este café sabe a chocolate.
This coffee tastes like chocolate.

sabor m.   *flavor*
El chocolate es mi sabor favorito.
Chocolate is my favorite flavor.

sabroso/-a   *tasty, delicious*
A todo el mundo le gusta la comida sabrosa.
Everybody likes tasty food.

sacacorchos m.   *corkscrew*
¿Tienes un sacacorchos?
Do you have a corkscrew?

sacar   *to take out, to extract*
Necesito sacar el corcho de esta botella.
I need to take out this bottle's cork.

sacerdote m.   *priest*
Los sacerdotes aztecas practicaban sacrificios humanos en las
    pirámides.
Aztec priests practiced human sacrifice on the pyramids.

saco (de dormir) m.   *sack/sleeping bag*
En la playa es mejor una hamaca que un saco de dormir.
At the beach a hammock is better than a sleeping bag.

sala (de espera) f.   *living room, (waiting room)*
Por favor espere en la sala de espera.
Please wait in the waiting room.

salado/-a   *salty*
El pescado estaba muy salado.
The fish was very salty.

salario m.   *salary, wage*
Muchas veces el salario mínimo es insuficiente para cubrir
   necesidades básicas.
Minimum wage is often insufficient to cover basic needs.

saldo (bancario) m.   *(bank) account balance*
Comprar demasiadas cosas no sería bueno para mi saldo
   bancario.
Buying too many things wouldn't be good for my account balance.

salida (del sol) f.   *exit, departure, sunrise*
Las salidas de emergencia están claramente señaladas.
The emergency exits are clearly marked.

salir   *to exit, to go out*
¿Quieres salir conmigo?
Do you want to go out with me?

salón (de clase)   *lounge, (class)room*
Mi salón de clase es muy frío en el invierno.
My classroom is very cold in the winter.

saltar   *to jump, to leap*
Salto la cuerda para ejercitarme.
I jump rope for exercise.

salto m.   *jump, leap*
No des un salto sin ver dónde caerás.
Don't take a leap without looking where you'll fall.

saludar   *to greet*
En muchos países la gente se saluda con un beso.
In many countries people greet each other with a kiss.

salvar(se)   *to save, to rescue*
Nos salvó la campana.
We were saved by the bell.

salvavidas m. & f.   *lifesaver, lifeguard*
Es más seguro nadar cuando hay un salvavidas.
It's safer to swim when there's a lifeguard.

santo/-a (adj.) *holy/*(n.) *saint*
El culto a los santos es tan importante en España como en
Latinoamérica.
The cult of saints is as important in Spain as it is in Latin America.

sartén m. *frying pan*
Necesitamos dos cacerolas y un sartén.
We need two sauce pans and a frying pan.

sastre m. *tailor*
¿Conoces un sastre que me pueda arreglar estos pantalones?
Do you know a tailor who can fix these pants for me?

satisfecho/-a *satisfied, content*
La comida me dejó muy satisfecho.
The meal left me very satisfied.

secadora (de pelo) f. *(hair)dryer*
¿Puedo conectar mi secadora de pelo?
Can I plug in my hair dryer?

secar(se) *to dry (up)*
Necesito secar mi ropa.
I need to dry my clothes.

sección (de [no] fumar) f. *([non]-smoking) section*
¿Prefiere la sección de fumar o de no fumar?
Do you prefer the smoking or the non-smoking section?

seco/-a *dry*
Ya está seca tu ropa.
Your clothes are dry now.

secreto m. *secret*
El secreto de la salsa está en la mezcla de los condimentos.
The secret of the sauce is in the condiment blend.

sed f. *thirst*
Tengo sed.
I am thirsty.

seda f. *silk*
No me gustan las sábanas de seda.
I don't like silk sheets.

seguir   *to follow, to continue*
Sígueme.
Follow me.

según   *according to*
Según este mapa, estamos por llegar.
According to this map, we are about to get there.

segunda clase f.   *second class*
Quiero comprar un boleto de segunda clase a Cuernavaca.
I want to buy a second-class ticket to Cuernavaca.

seguridad f.   *security*
Llamaré a seguridad.
I will call security.

seguro (médico, de vida, social) m.   *(medical, life) insurance,*
   medical insurance, social security
¿Tienes un seguro médico?
Do you have medical insurance?

seguro/-a   *safe*
Me siento más seguro en grupo.
I feel safer in a group.

seleccionar   *to select, to pick*
Hay que seleccionar los ingredientes más frescos.
We have to select the freshest ingredients.

sello postal m.   *postage stamp*
¿Cuántos sellos postales se necesitan para enviar esta carta a los
   Estados Unidos?
How many postage stamps are needed to mail this letter to the U.S.?

selva f.   *jungle*
Para llegar a estas ruinas tendremos que atravesar la selva.
To get to these ruins we'll have to go through the jungle.

semáforo m.   *traffic light*
Respeta los semáforos si no quieres tener un accidente.
Respect the traffic lights if you don't want to have an accident.

sembrar   *to plant*
Mi tío siembra vegetales en su huerta cada año.
My uncle plants vegetables in his vegetable garden every year.

semejante   *similar*
Este modelo es semejante pero más barato.
This model is similar but cheaper.

semilla f.   *seed*
Mi tío usa solamente semillas orgánicas.
My uncle uses only organic seeds.

señal f.   *signal, sign*
Obedece todas las señales de tránsito.
Obey all the traffic signals.

señalar   *to signal, to point to, to point out*
El guía iba señalando los detalles interesantes.
The guide kept pointing out the interesting details.

sencillo/-a   *simple, easy*
Es más sencillo llegar al museo en metro.
It's easier to get to the museum on the subway.

sendero m.   *path*
Este es el sendero que conduce a las ruinas de que te hablé.
This is the path to the ruins I told you about.

señor(a)   *Mr., sir/Mrs., madam, lady*
Esa señora es la esposa del señor López.
That lady is Mr. López's wife.

señorita f.   *young woman, Miss*
Su hija es una señorita muy talentosa.
Their daughter is a very talented young lady.

sensato/-a   *sensible*
Si eres sensato no tendrás ningún problema durante el viaje.
If you're sensible you will not have any trouble during the trip.

sensibilidad f.   *sensitivity, feeling, sensibility*
Algunos asuntos deben tratarse con gran sensibilidad.
Some matters must be addressed with great sensitivity.

sensual   *sensual, sensuous*
Los ritmos latinos en general son muy sensuales.
Latin rhythms in general are very sensual.

sentar(se)   *to sit down*
Siéntense, por favor.
Please, sit down.

sentido m.   *sense, meaning, direction*
Esta comedia no tiene sentido.
The comedy (play) doesn't make sense.

sentimiento m.   *feeling*
Los sentimientos pueden ser más poderosos que la razón.
Feelings can be more powerful than reason.

sentir(se)   *to feel*
Me siento culpable por lo que hice.
I feel guilty for what I did.

separar(se)   *to separate*
No se separen del grupo para no perderse.
Don't separate yourselves from the group so you don't get lost.

ser   *to be* (as masculine noun), *being*
¿Ser o no ser? Esa es la pregunta.
To be or not to be? That is the question.

serie f.   *series*
Una serie de medidas coordinadas es necesaria para manejar la
crisis del SIDA.
*A series of coordinated measures is necessary to manage the AIDS
crisis.*

serio/-a   *serious*
El SIDA es otra amenaza global muy seria.
AIDS is another very serious global threat.

seropositivo/-a   *HIV positive*
En la actualidad hay más opciones médicas para las personas
seropositivas.
Today there are more medical options for people who are HIV positive.

servicio (de mesa) m.   *(table) service*
El servicio en ese hotel no es muy bueno.
The service at that hotel isn't very good.

servicios m. pl.   *restrooms*
¿Puede decirme dónde están los servicios?
Can you tell me where the restrooms are?

servilleta f.   *napkin*
Las servilletas de papel no son elegantes pero son prácticas.
Paper napkins aren't elegant but they are practical.

servir(se)   *to serve*
El mesero nos sirvió la comida rápidamente.
The waiter served us the food quickly.

sexo m.   *sex*
Hay que practicar sexo seguro para evitar contagiarse de SIDA.
Safe sex must be practiced in order to avoid getting AIDS.

si   *if*
Si llueve no podremos ir de excursión.
If it rains we can't go on the excursion.

sí   *yes*
Sí, tienes razón.
Yes, you're right.

SIDA m.   *AIDS*
Encontrar una vacuna contra el SIDA es sólo una cuestión de
tiempo.
Finding an AIDS vaccine is only a matter of time.

siempre   *always*
Siempre como pan tostado en el desayuno.
I always eat toast for breakfast.

siesta f.   *nap*
Es saludable tomar una siesta.
It's healthy to take a nap.

siglo m.   *century*
Este edificio es del siglo dieciséis.
This building dates to the sixteenth century.

significado m.   *meaning*
Este lugar tiene mucho significado para mí.
This place has a lot of meaning for me.

siguiente   *next, following*
Necesitamos bajar en la siguiente estación.
We need to get off at the next station.

silencio m.   *silence*
A veces el silencio dice más que las palabras.
Sometimes silence says more than words.

silla f.   *chair*
La mesa del comedor tiene doce sillas.
The dining-room table has twelve chairs.

sillón m.   *armchair*
Los sillones son más cómodos que las sillas.
Armchairs are more comfortable than chairs.

similar   *similar*
Estos modelos son similares pero éste es mucho más barato.
These models are similar but this one is a lot cheaper.

simpático/-a   *nice, friendly*
Ignacio es muy simpático.
Ignacio is very nice.

sin (embargo)   *without, (nevertheless)*
No quiero ir sin ti.
I don't want to go without you.

sinceridad f.   *sincerity*
La sinceridad es la marca de un verdadero amigo.
Sincerity is the mark of a true friend.

sintético/-a   *synthetic*
Mi tío nunca usa fertilizantes sintéticos en su huerta.
My uncle never uses synthetic fertilizers in his vegetable garden.

sistema m.   *system*
La huerta es sólo un hobby, en realidad mi tío es analista de sistemas.
The vegetable garden is only a hobby, in fact my uncle is a systems analyst.

sitio m.   *place, site*
Conozco un sitio agradable para comer.
I know a nice place to eat.

sobre   *on (top of)/(as masculine noun), envelope*
El sobre está sobre la mesa.
The envelope is on the table.

sobredosis f.   *overdose*
Una sobredosis puede ser mortal.
An overdose can be deadly.

sobrenatural   *supernatural*
¿Crees en los fenómenos sobrenaturales?
Do you believe in supernatural phenomena?

sobrio/-a   *sober*
Hay que estar sobrio para manejar.
You have to be sober to drive.

sol m.   *sun*
Los incas adoraban al sol.
The Incas worshipped the sun.

solamente   *only*
Solamente tomo café en las mañanas.
I only drink coffee in the mornings.

soldado m. & f.   *soldier*
Los soldados desfilan el día de la independencia.
Soldiers parade on Independence Day.

soleado/-a   *sunny*
Me gustan los días soleados.
I like sunny days.

solicitar   *to request*
Solicitaré una visa para viajar a Cuba.
I will request a visa to travel to Cuba.

solo   *alone*
Viajar solo no es tan divertido.
Traveling alone is not as much fun.

sólo   *only*
Sólo he estado fuera del país una vez.
I've only been out of the country once.

soltero/-a   *single (bachelor/spinster)*
Ester no está casada; es soltera.
Ester is not married; she is single.

sombra f.   *shadow*
Sentémonos a la sombra del árbol.
Let's sit down under the tree's shadow.

soñar   *to dream*
¿Qué soñaste anoche?
What did you dream last night?

sonido m.   *sound*
Me gusta el sonido del mar.
I like the sound of the sea.

sonreír   *to smile*
¡Sonrían para la foto!
Smile for the picture!

sonrisa f.   *smile*
Las sonrisas son mejores que las lágrimas.
Smiles are better than tears.

sordo/-a   *deaf*
Mi abuelo está un poco sordo.
My grandfather is a little deaf.

sorprendente   *surprising, amazing*
La tecnología actual es sorprendente.
Current technology is amazing.

sorprender   *to surprise*
Sorprendí a Raúl con un regalo.
I surprised Raúl with a gift.

sorpresa f.   *surprise*
Este viaje ha estado lleno de sorpresas.
This trip has been full of surprises.

sospechoso/-a   *suspicious*
Cuidado con los tipos sospechosos.
Beware of suspicious types.

sótano m.   *basement*
Las maletas están en el sótano.
The luggage is in the basement.

suave   *soft, smooth*
¡Qué sábanas tan suaves!
What soft sheets!

subida f.   *ascent*
La subida a la montaña fue difícil.
The ascent up the mountain was difficult.

subir(se)   *to go up, to climb*
¿Quieres subirte a la montaña rusa?
Do you want to ride the roller coaster?

sucio/-a *dirty*
El piso de la cocina está muy sucio.
The kitchen floor is very dirty.

sudar *to perspire, to sweat*
Cuando hago ejercicio sudo.
When I exercise I sweat.

suelo m. *ground, floor*
La taza cayó al suelo y se rompió en mil pedazos.
The cup fell to the floor and broke into a thousand pieces.

sueño m. *dream, sleep*
Los sueños se pueden hacer realidad.
Dreams can come true.

suerte f. *luck*
Te deseo buena suerte.
I wish you good luck.

suficiente *enough, sufficient*
No olvides traer suficiente agua.
Don't forget to bring enough water.

sufrir *to suffer*
Sufrió una contusión al caer.
He suffered a contusion when he fell.

sugerencia f. *suggestion*
¿Puedo hacerte una sugerencia?
May I make a suggestion?

sugerir *to suggest*
Te sugiero que no empaques demasiado.
I suggest you don't pack too much.

sur m. *south*
Argentina está en el extremo sur del continente.
Argentina is in the southern-most extreme of the continent.

T

tabaco m. *tobacco*
El mejor tabaco viene del Caribe.
The best tobacco comes from the Caribbean.

tal vez   *maybe, perhaps*
Tal vez no te guste lo que compré para ti.
Perhaps you won't like what I bought for you.

talco m.   *baby powder*
El talco es bueno para evitar el pie de atleta.
Baby powder is good for avoiding athlete's foot.

talla f.   *size (clothing)*
¿Tiene este vestido en una talla más grande?
Do you have this dress in a larger size?

taller m.   *repair shop, garage*
¿Hay un taller mecánico cerca de aquí?
Is there a garage near here?

tamaño m.   *size*
¿De qué tamaño es la cama? Es tamaño matrimonial.
What size is the bed? It's a double.

también   *also, as well*
Agustín trabaja y estudia también.
Agustín works and studies as well.

tampoco   *neither*
La visita no fue interesante, ni divertida tampoco.
The visit was neither interesting nor fun.

tapa f.   *lid*
No encuentro la tapa de la botella de champú.
I can't find the shampoo-bottle's lid.

tapar(se)   *to cover (up)*
Tápate bien para que no te dé frío.
Cover up so you don't get cold.

tapete m.   *rug*
El tapete de la sala está muy sucio.
The living-room rug is very dirty.

tapón m.   *plug*
Necesito un tapón para la bañera.
I need a plug for the bathtub.

taquilla f.   *box office, ticket counter*
¿Dónde está la taquilla del teatro?
Where is the theater box office?

tardar(se)   *to take time, to be long*
Si tardamos mucho no llegaremos a tiempo.
If we take too long we won't get there on time.

tarea f.   *chore, homework*
Trapear el piso de la cocina es una tarea necesaria.
Mopping the kitchen floor is a necessary chore.

tarifa f.   *rate, fare*
¿Cuál es la tarifa por hora?
What's the hourly rate?

tarjeta (de crédito, postal) f.   *(credit, post) card*
Mándame una tarjeta postal.
Send me a postcard.

taxi m.   *taxi*
¿Me puede llamar un taxi?
Can you call me a taxi?

taza (del baño) f.   *cup/(toilet bowl)*
¿Quieres una taza de té?
Would you like a cup of tea?

tazón m.   *bowl*
Prefiero tomar mi sopa en un tazón.
I prefer to have my soup in a bowl.

teatro m.   *theater*
¿Quieres ir al cine o al teatro esta noche?
Do you want to go to the movies or to the theater tonight?

techo m.   *ceiling, roof*
Desde el techo se puede ver todo el valle.
From the roof you can see the whole valley.

teclado m.   *keyboard*
Los pianos y las computadoras tienen un teclado.
Pianos and computers have a keyboard.

tela f.   *cloth*
La tela de este vestido es de muy alta calidad.
This dress's cloth is very high quality.

teléfono (celular, móvil) m. *telephone, (cell phone)*
No olvides tu teléfono celular.
Do not forget your cell phone.

telenovela f. *soap opera*
Las telenovelas colombianas son populares en todo el mundo.
Colombian soap operas are popular all over the world.

televisión f. *television*
A pesar de tantos canales casi nunca hay nada que ver en la televisión.
In spite of so many channels, there is almost never anything to watch on TV.

temer *to fear*
No le temo a nada.
I fear nothing.

temperatura f. *temperature*
¿Qué temperatura máxima se espera para mañana?
What's the expected high temperature for tomorrow?

templado/-a *warm, mild*
Un día templado es ideal para una excursión larga.
A warm day is ideal for a long excursion.

templo m. *temple*
Muchos templos aztecas fueron destruidos por los conquistadores españoles.
Many Aztec temples were destroyed by the Spanish conquistadors.

temporada f. *season*
Los hoteles son más caros durante la temporada de turistas.
Hotels are more expensive during the tourist season.

temprano *early*
Mañana saldremos muy temprano por la mañana.
Tomorrow we will leave very early in the morning.

tenaz *stubborn, tenacious*
Al final, las personas tenaces alcanzan sus metas.
In the end, tenacious people reach their goals.

tenedor m. *fork*
¿Me puede traer un tenedor limpio?
Can you bring me a clean fork?

tener (que, calor, ganas)   *to have, (to have to, to feel hot, to feel like)*
No tengo ganas de ir pero tengo que hacerlo de todos modos.
I don't feel like going but I have to anyway.

terminal (de autobuses) f.   *(bus) terminal*
¿Me puede decir dónde está la terminal de autobuses?
Can you tell me where the bus terminal is?

terminar   *to finish, to end*
Tengo que terminar mi tarea antes de salir.
I need to finish my homework before going out.

terraza f.   *terrace*
¿Prefieren una mesa en la terraza?
Do you prefer a table on the terrace?

terremoto m.   *earthquake*
El terremoto de 1985 en la Ciudad de México fue terrible.
The 1985 earthquake in Mexico City was terrible.

terrible   *terrible*
Las consecuencias del calentamiento global serán cada vez más
terribles.
The consequences of global warming will be increasingly terrible.

tesoro m.   *treasure*
Todavía debe de haber tesoros de piratas en el fondo del Caribe.
There must still be pirate treasures at the bottom of the Caribbean.

testarudo/-a   *stubborn*
A veces las personas testarudas consiguen lo que quieren.
Sometimes stubborn people get what they want.

testigo m. & f.   *witness*
La policía interrogó a los testigos del accidente.
The police questioned the witnesses of the accident.

tibio/-a   *lukewarm*
Mi sopa está tibia.
My soup is lukewarm.

tienda (de abarrotes) f.   *(grocery) store*
¿Dónde está la tienda de abarrotes más cercana?
Where is the nearest grocery store?

tierno/-a   *tender, young, affectionate*
Rocío tiene un corazón muy tierno.
Rocío has a tender heart.

tierra f.   *earth, soil, ground*
Los tomates necesitan buena tierra y mucho sol para crecer.
Tomatoes need good soil and a lot of sun to grow.

tijeras f. pl.   *scissors*
¿Puedes prestarme unas tijeras?
Can you lend me some scissors?

timbre m.   *doorbell*
Creo que escuché sonar el timbre.
I think I heard the doorbell ring.

tímido/-a   *shy, timid*
Ser tímido no tiene prácticamente ninguna ventaja.
Being shy has practically no advantages.

tina f.   *tub*
Los baños no siempre tienen una tina.
Bathrooms don't always have a tub.

tinta f.   *ink*
Se le acabó la tinta a la impresora.
The printer ran out of ink.

típico/-a   *typical*
Estas artesanías son típicas de Oaxaca.
These handcrafts are typical of Oaxaca.

tipo (de cambio) m.   *type, (exchange rate)*
¿Cuál es el tipo de cambio hoy?
What is the exchange rate today?

tirar   *to throw (away)*
No tires a la basura las instrucciones; puedes necesitarlas.
Don't throw away the instructions; you might need them.

toalla f.   *towel*
Quisiera unas toallas limpias por favor.
I would like some clean towels please.

tocar   *to touch, to play (music)*
¿Sabes tocar un instrumento musical?
Do you know how to play a musical instrument?

todavía   *still, yet*
No estoy listo todavía.
I'm not ready yet.

todo(s)   *all, everyone, everything*
Todos quieren probar todos los platillos.
Everyone wants to try all the dishes.

tomar   *to take/to have something to eat or drink*
Toma tu sombrero y vamos a tomar una bebida cerca de la
    piscina.
Take your hat and let's go have a drink by the pool.

tonto/-a   *silly, dumb*
Me siento muy tonto por haberme perdido en un museo tan
    pequeño.
I feel silly for getting lost in such a small museum.

torcer(se)   *to twist*
Me caí y me torcí el brazo.
I fell down and twisted my arm.

torero m. & f.   *bullfighter*
Hay que ser muy valiente para ser torero.
You have to be very brave to be a bullfighter.

tormenta (eléctrica) f.   *(thunder) storm*
Se acerca una tormenta.
A storm is coming.

torpe   *clumsy*
Siempre me tropiezo porque soy muy torpe.
I always trip because I'm very clumsy.

torre f.   *tower*
No se puede subir a las torres de la catedral.
You can't go up the cathedral's towers.

tostada f.   *toast (Sp.)*
Para el desayuno, quiero una tostada con mantequilla y un café
    con leche.
For breakfast, I want a piece of toast with butter and coffee with milk.

trabajar   *to work*
¿Dónde trabajas?
Where do you work?

trabajo m.   *work, job*
Mi trabajo es peligroso.
My work is dangerous.

tradicional   *traditional*
Ese es el desayuno tradicional en España.
That's the typical breakfast in Spain.

traducir   *to translate*
Por favor tradúceme aquel anuncio.
Please translate that sign over there for me.

traductor(a)   *translator*
¿Crees que necesitaremos un traductor profesional?
Do you think that we will need a professional translator?

traer   *to bring*
No olvides traer un suéter por si hace frío.
Don't forget to bring a sweater in case it gets cold.

traficante de drogas m. & f.   *drug dealer*
La vida de un traficante de drogas no es tan glamorosa como
   parece.
A drug dealer's life is not as glamorous as it seems.

tráfico m.   *traffic*
El problema principal es que el tráfico de drogas es muy buen
   negocio.
The main problem is that drug trafficking is a very good business.

tragar   *to swallow*
Mastica bien antes de tragar para que no te atragantes.
Chew well before swallowing so you don't choke.

traición f.   *treason, betrayal*
Una traición puede destruir una relación.
A betrayal can destroy a relationship.

tramposo/-a m./f.   *cheater*
Al final, los tramposos sólo se engañan a sí mismos.
In the end, cheaters only cheat themselves.

tranquilo/-a   *calm, peaceful*
El mar está tranquilo; podemos nadar.
The sea is calm; we can swim.

transporte m.   *transport*
El tren es mi medio de transporte favorito.
The train is my favorite mode of transport.

tratar (de)   *to try (to)*
Vale la pena intentarlo una vez por lo menos.
It's worth trying at least once.

trato m.   *deal*
Hagamos un trato.
Let's make a deal.

travesura f.   *child's prank, mischief*
Los niños buenos no hacen travesuras.
Good children don't make mischief.

tren m.   *train*
Prefiero viajar en tren que en avión.
I would rather travel by train than by plane.

trepar   *to climb, to scale*
Tendremos que trepar un poco para llegar a las ruinas.
We will have to climb a little bit to get to the ruins.

tribunal m.   *court of law*
Si no respetas las leyes terminarás en un tribunal.
If you don't abide by the laws you will end up in a court of law.

triste   *sad*
¿Por qué estás triste?
Why are you sad?

tristeza f.   *sadness*
Es mejor la felicidad que la tristeza.
Happiness is better than sadness.

tropezar(se)   *to trip, to stumble*
Me tropecé con una piedra en el camino.
I tripped on a stone in the road.

trueno m.   *thunder*
Esos truenos anuncian una tormenta.
That thunder is announcing a storm.

tumba f.   *grave*
La pirámide principal de Palenque es la tumba de un rey.
The main pyramid at Palenque is a king's grave.

túnel m.   *tunnel*
Me asustan los túneles muy largos.
Long tunnels scare me.

turista m. & f.   *tourist*
No es lo mismo ser un turista que ser un viajero.
Being a tourist is not the same as being a traveler.

turístico/-a   *tourist*
Prefiero evitar los lugares turísticos.
I prefer to avoid tourist attractions.

U

último/-a   *last*
Mi último viaje a Guatemala fue fantástico.
My last trip to Guatemala was fantastic.

una vez f.   *once*
He estado en Costa Rica solamente una vez.
I have been in Costa Rica only once.

único/-a   *only, unique*
Es el único país que he visitado en Centroamérica.
It's the only country I have visited in Central America.

unidad (de disco) f.   *unit/(disk drive)*
¿Puede reparar la unidad de disco de mi computadora portátil?
Can you fix my laptop's disk drive?

uniforme m.   *uniform* (also adj.)
El uniforme de los burócratas es un traje y una corbata.
The uniform of bureaucrats is a suit and a tie.

unir(se)   *to unite, to join*
Me gustaría unirme a su grupo.
I would like to join your group.

universidad f.   *university*
Doy clases de español en la universidad de West Virginia.
I teach Spanish at West Virginia University.

urgente(mente)   *urgent(ly)*
Es urgente encontrar una solución al problema de la
     contaminación.
Finding a solution to the problem of pollution is urgent.

usado/-a   *worn, used*
Estos zapatos son muy cómodos porque están muy usados.
These shoes are very comfortable because they're very worn.

usar   *to use*
¿Puedo usar su baño?
May I use your bathroom?

utensilios m. pl.   *utensils*
Olvidamos traer utensilios así es que tendremos que comer con
los dedos.
We forgot to bring utensils so we will have to eat with our fingers.

útil   *useful*
Saber hablar español es muy útil.
Knowing Spanish is very useful.

V

vacaciones f. pl.   *vacation, holiday*
¿A dónde van a ir de vacaciones?
Where are you going on your vacation?

vacante f.   *vacancy* (as adj.) *vacant*
No encontramos ningún asiento vacante.
We didn't find any vacant seats.

vacío/-a   *empty*
El avión estaba casi vacío.
The plane was almost empty.

vagón (de tren) m.   *train car*
Todos los asientos del vagón estaban ocupados.
All the seats in the train car were taken.

valiente   *brave*
No tienes que ser valiente si eres listo.
You don't have to be brave if you're smart.

valija f.   *suitcase*
Viajo con una valija pequeña.
I travel with a small suitcase.

valioso/-a   *valuable*
No traigas nada valioso.
Don't bring anything valuable.

valle m.   *valley*
Desde este mirador se puede ver todo el valle de Oaxaca.
From this lookout you can see the whole Oaxaca Valley.

valor m.   *value/courage, bravery*
A veces hay que mostrar valor.
Sometimes you have to show courage.

vanidoso/-a   *vain*
A las personas vanidosas les gusta verse en el espejo.
Vain people like looking at themselves in the mirror.

variar   *to vary*
El precio de la moneda varía según el mercado.
The price of currency varies according to the market.

varios   *several, various*
Vamos a visitar varios museos en Madrid.
We are going to visit several museums in Madrid.

vaso m.   *(drinking) glass*
¿Quieres un vaso de agua?
Do you want a glass of water?

vecindario m.   *neighborhood*
El hotel está en un vecindario agradable.
The hotel is in a nice neighborhood.

vecino/-a m./f.   *neighbor*
Nuestros vecinos nos invitaron a su fiesta.
Our neighbors invited us to their party.

vegetariano/-a   *vegetarian*
Soy vegetariano.
I am a vegetarian.

vehículo m.   *vehicle*
Necesitamos un vehículo rápido para llegar pronto.
We need a fast vehicle to get there quickly.

vela f.   *candle*
Aquí están las velas, ¿dónde están los cerillos?
Here are the candles, where are the matches?

velocidad f.   *speed*
Respeta el límite de velocidad.
Respect the speed limit.

vencer   *to defeat, to win, to vanquish*
El equipo local venció al equipo visitante.
The home team defeated the visiting team.

vender   *to sell*
¿Dónde venden artesanías?
Where do they sell handcrafts?

veneno m.   *poison*
El veneno de algunas serpientes es mortal.
The poison of some snakes is deadly.

venenoso/-a   *poisonous*
Es útil saber identificar las serpientes venenosas.
Knowing how to identify poisonous snakes is useful.

venir   *to come*
Ven a almorzar con nosotros.
Come have lunch with us.

venta f.   *sale*
Esta casa está a la venta.
This house is for sale.

ventaja f.   *advantage*
Viajar en tren tiene muchas ventajas.
Traveling by train has many advantages.

ventana f.   *window*
Cierra la ventana por favor
Close the window please.

ventilador m.   *fan*
Tengo calor, ¿puedes encender el ventilador?
I'm hot; can you turn on the fan?

ver   *to see, to watch*
No me gusta ver la televisión.
I don't like to watch television.

verdad f.   *truth*
Dime la verdad.
Tell me the truth.

verificar   *to verify*
Los agentes de inmigración están ahí para verificar la identidad
de los viajeros.
Immigration agents are there to verify travelers' identities.

vestíbulo m.   *lobby*
Te esperaré en el vestíbulo del hotel.
I will wait for you in the hotel lobby.

vestir(se)   *to dress, to get dressed*
Luis siempre se viste muy bien.
Luis always dresses very well.

veraz   *truthful*
En los negocios, como en el amor, es mejor ser veraz.
In business, as in love, it's better to be truthful.

vez f.   *time (instance)*
Generalmente, se come tres veces al día.
In general, people eat three times a day.

viajar   *to travel*
Me encanta viajar en tren.
I love to travel by train.

viaje (de negocios) m.   *(business) trip*
¿Es un viaje de negocios o una vacación?
Is it a business trip or a vacation?

viajero/-a m./f.   *traveler*
Hay muchos viajeros en esta época del año.
There are many travelers this time of year.

vida f.   *life*
Todo el mundo quiere una buena vida.
Everybody wants a good life.

videograbadora f.   *video recorder*
Olvidé mi videograbadora en casa.
I forgot my video recorder at home.

videojuego m.   *video/computer game*
Los videojuegos son muy populares hoy en día.
Video games are very popular these days.

viejo/-a   *old, old man/woman*
Mi maleta es muy vieja; necesito una nueva.
My suitcase is very old; I need a new one.

viento m.   *wind*
El viento está soplando fuertemente.
The wind is blowing hard.

violencia f.   *violence*
El tráfico de drogas genera mucha violencia de los dos lados de la frontera.
Drug trafficking generates a lot of violence on both sides of the border.

virus m.   *virus*
No hay una cura efectiva contra los virus.
There isn't an effective cure against viruses.

visa (de negocios) f.   *(business) visa*
No se necesita una visa para viajar a España o a México.
You don't need a visa to travel to Spain or Mexico.

visitar   *to visit*
Vale la pena visitar las ruinas de Palenque.
The Palenque ruins are worth visiting.

vista f.   *view/eyesight*
Desde mi ventana tengo una vista hermosa.
From my window I have a beautiful view.

víveres m. pl.   *food supplies*
Debemos llevar algunos víveres para la excursión.
We must take some food supplies for the excursion.

vivir   *to live*
¿Alguien vive aquí?
Does anybody live here?

volar   *to fly*
Vuelo seguido a Monterrey por negocios.
I fly to Monterrey often for business.

voluntad f. *will*
Si tienes la voluntad de hacerlo, lo harás.
If you have the will to do it, you will.

volver(se) *to return, to become*
Quiero volver a Ecuador pronto.
I want to return to Ecuador soon.

voz f. *voice*
¿Puedes oír mi voz?
Can you hear my voice?

vuelo f. *flight*
El vuelo llegó a tiempo.
The flight arrived on time.

vuelta f. *turn/tour/return*
Da vuelta a la derecha en la próxima esquina.
Turn right at the next corner.

Y

y *and*
Compré un vestido y un par de zapatos
I bought a dress and a pair of shoes.

ya *already*
¿Ya has visto la exposición de Picasso?
Have you already seen the Picasso exhibition?

Z

zambullir(se) *to plunge*
No te zambullas de cabeza en un lago.
Don't plunge headfirst into a lake.

zanja (de drenaje) f. *(drainage) ditch*
Mi tío cavó una zanja para regar su huerta.
My uncle dug a ditch to water his vegetable garden.

zócalo m. *central/main square*
En el zócalo hay una estatua del héroe nacional.
On the main square there is a statue of the national hero.

zona f.   *zone*
Esta zona arqueológica todavía no está totalmente estudiada.
This archaeological zone isn't fully studied yet.

zoológico m.   *zoo*
¿Quieres visitar el zoológico?
Do you want to visit the zoo?

zurdo/-a   *left-handed*
Tristán es zurdo.
Tristan is left-handed.

Category Section

ANIMALES	m. pl.	ANIMALS
abeja	f.	*bee*
araña	f.	*spider*
burro/-a	m./f.	*donkey*
caballo/yegua	m./f.	*horse/mare*
cabra	f.	*goat*
cerdo/-a	m./f.	*pig, pork*
conejo/-a	m./f.	*rabbit*
cucaracha	f.	*cockroach*
cuervo	m.	*crow*
culebra	f.	*water snake*
gallo/gallina	m./f.	*hen/rooster*
gato/-a	m./f.	*cat*
hormiga	f.	*ant*
lagarto	m.	*lizard*
lobo/-a	m./f.	*wolf*
mono/-a	m./f.	*monkey*
mosca	f.	*fly*
mosquito	m.	*mosquito*
oso/-a	m./f.	*bear*

oveja	f.	*sheep*
pájaro	m.	*bird*
palomo/-a	m./f.	*pigeon/dove*
pato/-a	m./f.	*duck*
pavo/-a	m./f.	*turkey*
perro/-a	m./f.	*dog*
puerco/-a	m./f.	*pig, pork*
rana	f.	*frog*
ratón	m.	*mouse*
tiburón	m.	*shark*
toro/vaca	m./f.	*bull/cow*
víbora	f.	*snake*

EL CUERPO	m.	***THE BODY***
barba	f.	*beard*
barbilla	f.	*chin*
bigote	m.	*moustache*
boca	f.	*mouth*
brazo	m.	*arm*
cabeza	f.	*head*
cadera	f.	*hip*
cara	f.	*face*
ceja	f.	*eyebrow*
cerebro	m.	*brain*
cintura	f.	*waist*
codo	m.	*elbow*

corazón	m.	*heart*
costilla	f.	*rib*
cuello	m.	*neck*
dedo (del pie)	m.	*finger, toe*
diente	m.	*tooth*
espalda	f.	*back*
estómago	m.	*stomach*
garganta	f.	*throat*
hombro	m.	*shoulder*
hueso	m.	*bone*
labio	m.	*lip*
lengua	f.	*tongue*
mandíbula	f.	*jaw*
mano	f.	*hand*
nalgas	f. pl.	*buttocks*
nariz	f.	*nose*
ojo	m.	*eye*
oreja	f.	*ear*
panza	f.	*belly, stomach*
pecho	m.	*chest, breast*
pelo	m.	*hair*
pene	m.	*penis*
pie	m.	*foot*
pierna	f.	*leg*
pulmón	m.	*lung*
rodilla	f.	*knee*

sangre	f.	*blood*
tobillo	m.	*ankle*
vagina	f.	*vagina*
ROPA	f.	***CLOTHES***
abrigo	m.	*overcoat*
arete	m.	*earring*
blusa	f.	*blouse*
bolsillo	m.	*pocket*
bufanda	f.	*scarf*
calcetín	m.	*sock*
calzado	m.	*footwear*
calzoncillos/ calzones	m. pl.	*underpants/briefs*
chaqueta	f.	*jacket*
collar	m.	*necklace*
corbata	f.	*necktie*
falda	f.	*skirt*
gorra	f.	*cap*
guante	m.	*glove*
impermeable	m.	*raincoat*
medias	f. pl.	*stockings*
saco	m.	*jacket (L. Am.)*
sandalias	f. pl.	*sandals*
sombrero	m.	*hat*
sostén	m.	*bra*

traje (de baño)	m.	*(bathing) suit*
vestido	m.	*dress*
zapatos (tenis)	m. pl.	*(tennis) shoes*

COLORES — m. pl. — *COLORS*

amarillo	*yellow*
anaranjado	*orange*
azul (claro, oscuro)	*(light, dark) blue*
blanco	*white*
café	*brown*
gris	*grey*
marrón	*brown*
morado	*purple*
negro	*black*
rojo	*red*
rosa	*pink*
verde	*green*

LA FAMILIA — f. — *THE FAMILY*

abuelo/-a	m./f.	*grandfather/mother*
cuñado/-a	m./f.	*brother/sister-in-law*
esposo/-a	m./f.	*husband/wife, spouse*
hermano/-a	m./f.	*brother/sister*
hijo/-a	m./f.	*son/daughter*
madre	f.	*mother*
madrina	f.	*godmother*

nieto/-a	m./f.	*grandson/daughter*
nuera	f.	*daughter-in-law*
padre	m.	*father*
padrino	m.	*godfather*
primo/-a	m./f.	*cousin*
sobrino/-a	m./f.	*nephew/niece*
suegro/-a	m./f.	*father/mother-in-law*
tío/-a	m./f.	*uncle/aunt*
yerno	m.	*son-in-law*

COMIDA	f.	***FOOD***
Frutas y Verduras	f. pl.	***Fruits & Vegetables***
aceituna	f.	*olive*
aguacate	m.	*avocado*
ajo	m.	*garlic*
albaricoque	m.	*apricot (Sp.)*
alcachofa	f.	*artichoke*
apio	m.	*celery*
berenjena	f.	*eggplant*
brócoli	m.	*broccoli*
calabacita	f.	*zucchini*
calabaza	f.	*pumpkin*
cebolla	f.	*onion*
cereza	f.	*cherry*
chabacano	m.	*apricot (L. Am.)*
champiñón	m.	*mushroom*

chile	m.	*chili pepper*
ciruela	f.	*plum*
coco	m.	*coconut*
col	f.	*cabbage*
coliflor	f.	*cauliflower*
durazno	m.	*peach*
espárrago	m.	*asparagus*
espinaca	f.	*spinach*
frambuesa	f.	*raspberry*
fresa	f.	*strawberry*
frijoles	m. pl.	*beans (L. Am.)*
fruta	f.	*fruit*
frutilla	f.	*strawberry (L.Am.)*
garbanzo	m.	*chickpea*
guisante	m.	*pea*
habichuelas	f. pl.	*beans*
higo	m.	*fig*
hongo	m.	*mushroom*
lechuga	f.	*lettuce*
legumbre	f.	*vegetable*
lentejas	f. pl.	*lentils*
limón	m.	*lemon*
mandarina	f.	*tangerine*
manzana	f.	*apple*
melocotón	m.	*peach (Sp.)*
naranja	f.	*orange*
papa/patata (Sp.)	f.	*potato*

papas/patatas fritas	f. pl.	*French fries*
pasa	f.	*raisin*
pepino	m.	*cucumber*
pera	f.	*pear*
pimiento verde	m.	*green pepper*
piña	f.	*pineapple*
plátano	f.	*banana*
pomelo	m.	*grapefruit (Sp.)*
puré (de papa, de patatas)	m.	*purée, mashed potatoes*
rábano	m.	*radish*
sandía	f.	*watermelon*
tomate	m.	*tomato*
toronja	f.	*grapefruit (L.Am.)*
uva	f	*grape*
zanahoria	f.	*carrot*
Huevos y Lácteos	m. pl.	***Eggs & Dairy***
crema (batida)	f.	*(whipped) cream (L. Am.)*
helado	m.	*ice cream*
huevo (revuelto, frito)	m.	*(scrambled, fried) egg*
leche (descremada)	f.	*(skim) milk*
mantequilla	f.	*butter*
margarina	f.	*margarine*
nata (montada)	f.	*(whipped) cream (Sp.)*
queso	m.	*cheese*
yema	f.	*egg yolk*

Carnes y Mariscos	m. pl.	*Meat & Seafood*
albóndigas	f. pl.	*meatballs*
almejas	f. pl.	*clams*
atún	m.	*tuna*
bacalao	m.	*haddock/cod, codfish*
barbacoa	f.	*barbecue*
calamares	m. pl.	*squid*
camarón	m.	*shrimp*
cangrejo	m.	*crab*
carne (de res, de cerdo)	f.	*meat (beef, pork)*
carnero	m.	*mutton*
carnitas	f. pl.	*diced pork meat (Mex.)*
chuleta	f.	*cutlet, chop*
churrasco	m.	*barbecued steak (Arg.)*
cordero	m.	*lamb*
filete	m.	*steak*
hamburguesa	f.	*hamburger*
jamón	m.	*ham*
langosta	f.	*lobster*
langostinos	m. pl.	*prawns*
lechón	m.	*suckling pig*
parrilla	f.	*barbecue grill*
pechuga	f.	*breast (fowl)*
pollo	m.	*chicken*
salchicha	f.	*sausage*

salchichón	m.	spiced sausage— similar to pepperoni or salami
ternera	f.	veal
tocino	m.	bacon
Otras Cosas	**f. pl.**	**Other Items**
aceite (de oliva)	m.	(olive) oil
almendra	f.	almond
almíbar	m.	syrup
aperitivo	m.	appetizer
arroz (con leche)	m.	rice (pudding)
asado/-a		roasted/barbecue (Arg.)
avena	f.	oats
azúcar	m.	sugar
bizcocho	m.	sponge cake
bocadillo	m.	snack, sandwich (Sp.)
cacahuate	m.	peanut
cacao	m.	cocoa
caldo (de pollo)	m.	(chicken) broth
canela	f.	cinnamon
céreal	m.	cereal
chicle	m.	chewing gum (Mex.)
chocolate	m.	chocolate
churro	m.	fritter
clara (de huevo)	f.	egg white
condimento	m.	condiment

empanizado/-a		*breaded*
emparedado (de queso)	m.	*(cheese) sandwich*
ensalada (de frutas)	f.	*(fruit) salad*
entremés	m.	*starter*
especias	f. pl.	*spices*
fideos	m. pl.	*noodles*
flan	m.	*custard*
frito/-a		*fried*
galleta	f.	*cookie, biscuit*
goma de mascar	f.	*chewing gum*
guisado	m.	*stew*
harina	f.	*flour*
hervido/-a		*boiled*
jalea	f.	*jelly*
maíz	m.	*corn*
manteca	f.	*lard*
masa	f.	*dough*
mayonesa	f.	*mayonnaise*
menta	f.	*peppermint*
mermelada	f.	*jam*
miel	f.	*honey*
mole poblano	m.	*spicy chocolate sauce (Mex.)*
mostaza	f.	*mustard*
nuez	f.	*walnut*
paella	f.	*saffron rice with chicken and seafood*

pan (de caja, integral)	m.	*(sliced, whole wheat) bread*
pastel	m.	*cake (Mex.)*
pimienta	f.	*pepper*
postre	m.	*dessert*
sal	f.	*salt*
salsa (de tomate)	f.	*sauce, ketchup*
sopa	f.	*soup*
tallarín	m.	*noodle*
tarta (de manzana)	f.	*(apple) pie*
torta	f.	*cake, sandwich (Mex.)*
tortilla	f.	*potato omelet (Sp.), corn flat bread (L. Am.)*
trigo	m.	*wheat*
vinagre	m.	*vinegar*
Bebidas	**f. pl.**	***Drinks, Beverages***
agua (potable, mineral)	f.	*(drinking, mineral) water*
café	m.	*coffee*
cerveza (embotellada)	f.	*(bottled) beer*
jugo	m.	*juice*
mate	m.	*type of tea popular in S. America*
refresco	m.	*cold drink*
sangría	f.	*red wine punch*
té	m.	*tea*

trago	m.	*drink*
vino (tinto/blanco)	m.	*(red/white) wine*
zumo	m.	*juice (Sp.)*
COMIDAS	**f. pl.**	***MEALS***
almuerzo	m.	*lunch*
cena	f.	*dinner, supper*
desayuno	m.	*breakfast*
merienda	f.	*snack, early/light supper (L. Am.)*
SALUD	**f.**	***HEALTH***
alergia	f.	*allergy*
ampolla	f.	*blister*
analgésico	m.	*painkiller*
ardor	m.	*burning pain*
calmante	f.	*painkiller*
catarro	m.	*cold (illness)*
cirugía	f.	*surgery*
cirujano	m. & f.	*surgeon*
comezón	f.	*itch*
consulta (externa)	f.	*medical examination/ out-patient clinic*
consultorio médico	m.	*doctor's office*
convalecer		*to recover*
curación	f.	*treatment, cure*
curar		*to cure, to heal, to treat*

curita	f.	*Band-Aid*
desmayarse		*to faint*
diagnóstico	m.	*diagnosis*
diarrea	f.	*diarrhea*
dislocar		*to dislocate*
doler		*to hurt, to ache*
dolor (de cabeza)	m.	*pain, headache*
dosis	f.	*dose*
enfermarse		*to get sick*
enfermedad	f.	*disease, illness*
enfermero/-a	m./f.	*nurse*
enfermo/-a		*sick*
estreñimiento	m.	*constipation*
fiebre	f.	*fever*
gripe	f.	*flu*
hemorragia	f.	*hemorrhage*
herida	f.	*wound, injury*
hinchado/-a		*swollen*
indigestión	f.	*indigestion*
infarto	m.	*heart attack*
inflamación	f.	*swelling*
inhalador	m.	*inhaler*
intoxicación (alimenticia)	f.	*(food) poisoning*
jaqueca	f.	*migraine*
jarabe (para la tos)	m.	*(cough) syrup*

jeringa	f.	*syringe*
lastimado/-a		*hurt, injured*
lastimar(se)		*to hurt (oneself)*
lesionado/-a		*hurt, injured*
lesionar(se)		*to injure (oneself)*
malestar	m.	*discomfort*
medicina (general)	f.	*medicine, general practice*
médico	m. & f.	*doctor*
moretón	m.	*bruise*
picadura (de dientes, de insecto)	f.	*sting (cavity, insect bite)*
picazón	f.	*itch*
primeros auxilios	m. pl.	*first aid*
quemadura (de sol)	f.	*(sun) burn*
receta (médica)	f.	*prescription*
resfriado	m.	*cold (illness)*
retortijón	m.	*(stomach) cramp*
saludable		*healthy*
sangrar		*to bleed*
sano/-a		*healthy*
torcedura	f.	*sprain*
tos	f.	*cough*
toser		*to cough*
urticaria	f.	*rash, hives*
venda	f.	*bandage*

NÚMEROS　　m. pl.　　　NUMBERS

cero	*zero*
uno	*one*
dos	*two*
tres	*three*
cuatro	*four*
cinco	*five*
seis	*six*
siete	*seven*
ocho	*eight*
nueve	*nine*
diez	*ten*
once	*eleven*
doce	*twelve*
trece	*thirteen*
catorce	*fourteen*
quince	*fifteen*
dieciséis	*sixteen*
diecisiete	*seventeen*
dieciocho	*eighteen*
diecinueve	*nineteen*
veinte	*twenty*
veintiuno	*twenty-one*
veintidós	*twenty-two*
treinta	*thirty*
treinta y uno	*thirty-one*
treinta y dos	*thirty-two*

cuarenta	*forty*
cincuenta	*fifty*
sesenta	*sixty*
setenta	*seventy*
ochenta	*eighty*
noventa	*ninety*
cien	*one hundred*
ciento uno	*one hundred and one*
ciento dos	*one hundred and two*
doscientos	*two hundred*
trescientos	*three hundred*
cuatrocientos	*four hundred*
quinientos	*five hundred*
seiscientos	*six hundred*
setecientos	*seven hundred*
ochocientos	*eight hundred*
novecientos	*nine hundred*
mil	*one thousand*
dos mil	*two thousand*
cien mil	*one hundred thousand*
millón m.	*million*
dos millones	*two million*

PALABRAS f. pl. **INTERROGATIVAS**	*QUESTION* *WORDS*
¿cómo?	*how?*
¿cuál(es)?	*which?*

¿cuándo?		*when?*
¿cuánto?		*how much*
¿cuántos/-as?		*how many?*
¿dónde?		*where?*
¿por qué?		*why?*

DEPORTES	m. pl.	***SPORTS***
arbitro	m. & f.	*referee*
baloncesto	m.	*basketball*
béisbol	m.	*baseball*
boliche/bolos	m./m. pl.	*bowling*
caña (de pescar)	f.	*(fishing) rod*
cancha (de tenis)	f.	*(tennis) court*
ciclismo	m.	*cycling*
corrida (de toros)	f.	*bullfight*
equitación	f.	*horse riding*
esquí acuático	m.	*waterskiing*
esquiar		*to ski*
fútbol (americano)	m.	*soccer, football*
lucha libre	f.	*wrestling*
natación	f.	*swimming*
tenis	m.	*tennis*

TIENDAS	f. pl.	***STORES***
barbería	f.	*barber shop*
cafetería	f.	*cafeteria*
carnicería	f.	*butcher shop*
farmacia	f.	*pharmacy, drugstore*

ferretería	f.	*hardware store*
florería	f.	*flower shop*
joyería	f.	*jewelry store*
lavandería	f.	*laundromat*
librería	f.	*bookstore*
panadería	f.	*bakery*
papelería	f.	*stationers, office supply store*
peluquería	f.	*hairdresser*
sastrería	f.	*tailor shop*
supermercado	m.	*supermarket*
tintorería	f.	*dry cleaner's*
zapatería	f.	*shoe store*

TIEMPO	m.	*TIME*
año	m.	*year*
anoche		*last night*
ayer		*yesterday*
hora	f.	*hour*
hoy		*today*
mañana	f.	*morning/tomorrow*
medianoche	f.	*midnight*
mediodía	m.	*noon*
noche	f.	*evening*
tarde	f.	*afternoon/late*

DÍAS DE LA SEMANA	f. pl.	*DAYS OF THE WEEK*
lunes		*Monday*

martes		Tuesday
miércoles		Wednesday
jueves		Thursday
viernes		Friday
sábado		Saturday
domingo		Sunday
semana (próxima)	f.	(next) week

MESES — m. pl. — *MONTHS*

enero	January
febrero	February
marzo	March
abril	April
mayo	May
junio	June
julio	July
agosto	August
septiembre	September
octubre	October
noviembre	November
diciembre	December

LAS ESTACIONES — m. pl. — *THE SEASONS*

primavera	f.	spring
verano	m.	summer
otoño	m.	autumn
invierno	m.	winter

Spanish Grammar Primer

This section offers some vocabulary tips and the most basic essentials of Spanish grammar. It is a helpful starting point for a beginner and can serve as a quick reference for a more advanced speaker.

Abstract grammar can be very helpful, but the best way to integrate language rules will always be through frequent real-life use. Listen to as much Spanish as you can (music, movies, and television are good resources), communicate in Spanish as often as you can, using the words in this book, and soon you won't need to think about the grammar at all.

Vocabulary Tips and Cognates

Cognates are words that derive from a common ancestor language. Most words in Spanish and many words in English come from Latin or Greek. As a result, there are a lot of words in English that are cognates of words in Spanish; most are easily recognizable. Since changes are slight and predictable, you can quickly expand your vocabulary in Spanish by taking note of the following:

1. Some words are the same in both languages (except that their pronunciation may vary): color, crisis, drama, error, general, horror, probable, tropical, . . .
2. Some words add an extra vowel to the English word: client**e**, evident**e**, ignorant**e**, important**e**, part**e**, artist**a**, pianist**a**, problem**a**, program**a**, contact**o**, perfect**o**, líquid**o**, . . . *
3. Many words ending in -ty in English end in **-tad** or **-dad** in Spanish: facul**tad**, liber**tad**, curiosi**dad**, socie**dad**, eterni**dad**, capaci**dad**, reali**dad**, clari**dad**, . . .

---

*Please don't make the error, often parodied in movies, of thinking that adding an "o" at the end of every word in a sentence makes it sound like Spanish. In fact, native Spanish speakers will likely consider this rude.

4. Many words ending in -y in English end in -ía, -ia, or -io (depending on gender, see below): compañía, geografía, historia, farmacia, diccionario, ordinario, . . . *

5. Words that end in -tion in English generally end in -ción in Spanish: nación, administración, acción, fricción, sección, emoción, combinación, contribución, . . .

6. Words that end in -ous in English often end in -oso in Spanish: generoso, famoso, precioso, delicioso, tedioso, contagioso, curioso, escandaloso, religioso, . . .

Gender, Number, and Agreement

In Spanish, most nouns are gendered. *Silla* (chair), *mesa* (table), *carne* (meat), *flor* (flower), *canción* (song), and *mano* (hand) are feminine. *Escritorio* (desk), *sombrero* (hat), *sobre* (envelope), *calor* (heat), *camión* (bus), and *clima* (weather) are masculine. In some cases, the gender of a noun will depend on the object to which it applies: *cantante* (singer) can be either feminine or masculine. Likewise, *orden* (order) is feminine when it refers to the order issued by an authority and masculine when it refers to the order of things.

Since a word's ending doesn't always reveal whether it is masculine or feminine, it's useful to look at its corresponding definite (*the*) or indefinite (*a*) article:

Articles	Definite (*the*)		Indefinite (*a/an/some*)	
	Masculine	Feminine	Masculine	Feminine
Singular	el	la	un	una
Plural	los	las	unos	unas

In Spanish, articles and adjectives belonging to a noun must agree in gender with the noun.

Esa flor azul es muy bonita.**   *That blue flower is very pretty.*
María es **una** cantante muy   *María is a very talented singer.*
talentosa.
Pedro es **un** cantante muy   *Pedro is a very talented singer.*
talentoso.

---

* In a few cases, cognates don't have exactly the same meaning in Spanish as they do in English: *policía* means "police" in Spanish; policy should be translated as *política*.

** Adjectives that end in -e or a consonant don't change on account of gender.

Likewise, nouns, adjectives, and articles must agree in number. In Spanish, plurality is expressed by adding an -**s** to words that end in a vowel and -**es** to nouns that end in a consonant:

Las flore**s** azul**es** son mis preferidas.	*Blue flowers are my favorite.*
Pedro y **María** son **unos** cantante**s** muy buenos.‡	*Pedro and María are very good singers.*

Pronouns

Pronouns in Spanish function mostly as they do in English; they are used to replace the subject or the objects in a sentence to improve speech flow. Since they are an essential part of everyday speech, it is important to know a few things about personal pronouns in Spanish.

Subject		Indirect Object		Direct Object		Reflexive Object[5]	
yo	*I*	me	*to me*	me	*me*	me	*myself*
tú	*you*	te	*to you*	te	*you*	te	*yourself*
usted[1]	*you (formal)*	le [se][4]	*to you, to him/ her, to it*	lo, la	*you (formal)*	se	*yourself, him/ herself, itself[6]*
él	*him*			lo	*him, it m.*		
ella[2]	*she*			la	*her, it f.*		
noso-tros/as	*we*	nos	*to us*	nos	*us*	nos	*ourselves*
voso-tros/as[3]	*you pl.*	os	*to you pl.*	os	*you pl.*	os	*your-selves*
ustedes	*you pl.*	les [se]	*to you, to them*	los, las	*you pl.*	se	*your-selves, them-selves*
ellos	*they m.*			los	*them m.*		
ellas	*they f.*			las	*them f.*		

‡ When there are both feminine and masculine individuals or objects in a group, masculine adjectives and articles are used.

TABLE NOTE **1.** **Usted** (Ud.) is a more formal way of addressing a second person; it is used to address people of a superior rank (elders, bosses, officials, etc.) and with new acquaintances. Formal address uses the verb forms and pronouns of the third person as a way of setting a respectful distance between speaker and addressee (see VERB CONJUGATION CHARTS section beginning on p. 206). Compare the following sentences:

Formal: ¿Cómo **está** (usted)?　　*How are you?*
No quiero molestar**lo**.　　　　*I don't want to bother you.*
Informal: ¿Cómo **estás** (tú)?　　*How are you?*
No quiero molestar**te**.　　　　*I don't want to bother you.*

　Usted is used systematically in Latin America where it is considered polite, but only sporadically in Spain.

TABLE NOTE **2.** Note that Spanish does not have an equivalent of the subject pronoun "it:"

Está lloviendo.　*It is raining.*　　¿Quién era?　　*Who was it?*

TABLE NOTE **3.** **Vosotros/as** and **Ustedes** are used to address a group (some English dialects use "you all" or "y'all" for the same purpose). **Vosotros/as** is only used in Spain.

TABLE NOTE **4.** Object pronouns can precede an active verb or be attached at the end of an infinitive, a gerund, or an affirmative command (see VERB section beginning on p. 210):

Quiero comer una manzana. >　**La** quiero comer. = Quiero comer**la**.
　I want to eat an apple. >　　　　*I want to eat it.*
Estoy comiendo una manzana. >　**La** estoy comiendo. = Estoy comiéndo**la**.
　I am eating an apple. >　　　　　*I am eating it.*
¡Come la manzana! > ¡Cóme**la**!　but　　¡No comas la manzana!
　　　　　　　　　　　　　　　　　　　> No **la** comas
　　Eat the apple. >　　　　*Eat it.*　　*Don't eat the apple.* >
　　　　　　　　　　　　　　　　　　　　Don't eat it.

Direct objects can appear in a sentence as either a noun or a pronoun but not both. However, indirect object pronouns <u>must be used</u> whether or not the indirect object noun appears in the sentence:

Pedro **me** da dinero (**a mí**).   *Pedro gives money to me.*
Juan **le** da flores **a María**.   *Juan gives flowers to Mary.*

When using two object pronouns, the indirect object pronoun <u>always</u> comes first:

Pedro **me lo** da.   *Pedro gives it to me.*

When combined with the direct object pronouns **lo**, **la**, **los**, or **las**, the indirect object pronoun **le** changes to **se**:

Juan **se las** da (a María).   *Juan gives **them to her** (to Mary).*

TABLE NOTE 5. As in English, **reflexive pronouns** are used to "reflect" or return the action expressed by the verb back upon the subject:

Me veo en el   *I see myself in the*   María **se** viste.   *María dresses*
espejo.   *mirror.*   *(herself).*

Common reflexive actions include getting up (*levantarse*), washing (*lavarse*) or bathing (*bañarse*), sitting (*sentarse*), lying down (*acostarse*), and falling asleep (*dormirse*). Sometimes reflexivity is added for emphasis or precision. Compare the following:

romper	*to break*	Rompiste la ventana.	*You broke the window.*
romper**se**	*to break*	**Te** rompiste la pierna.	*You broke **your** leg.*
dormir	*to sleep*	Juan está durmiendo.	*Juan is sleeping.*
dormir**se**	*to fall asleep*	Juan está durmién**dose**.	*Juan is falling asleep.*
ir	*to go*	Vamos al cine.	*Let's go to the movies.*
ir**se**	*to leave, to go away*	Vámo**nos** al cine.	*Let's leave for the movies.*

TABLE NOTE 6. In Spanish the pronoun **se** is very often used to express a passive or an impersonal action in which the object may assume the function of the subject (which creates a reflexive-like expression):

En México **se** habla español.   *Spanish is spoken in Mexico. / People speak Spanish in Mexico.*

No se debe desperdiciar agua.   *Water mustn't be wasted. / One mustn't waste water.*

Verb Conjugation Charts

Regular verbs, simple tenses*

Past "used to = was

Past — probability

| Infinitive | INDICATIVE | | | | | SUBJUNCTIVE | |
	Present	Preterit	Imperfect	Future	Conditional	Present	Past
hablar (*to talk*)	hablo	hablé	hablaba	hablaré	hablaría	hable	hablara
	hablas	hablaste	hablabas	hablarás	hablarías	hables	hablaras
hablando (*talking*)	habla	habló	hablaba	hablará	hablaría	hable	hablara
hablado (*talked*)	hablamos	hablamos	hablábamos	hablaremos	hablaríamos	hablemos	habláramos
	habláis	hablasteis	hablabais	hablaréis	hablaríais	habléis	hablarais
	hablan	hablaron	hablaban	hablarán	hablarían	hablen	hablaran
comer (*to eat*)	como	comí	comía	comeré	comería	coma	comiera
	comes	comiste	comías	comerás	comerías	comas	comieras
comiendo (*eating*)	come	comió	comía	comerá	comería	coma	comiera
comido (*eaten*)	comemos	comimos	comíamos	comeremos	comeríamos	comamos	comiéramos
	coméis	comisteis	comíais	comeréis	comeríais	comáis	comierais
	comen	comieron	comían	comerán	comerían	coman	comieran

---

*Regular verbs are predictable; note the patterns of the different tenses to master verb conjugation quickly.

vivir (to live)	vivo	viví	vivía	viviré	viviría	viva	viviera
	vives	viviste	vivías	vivirás	vivirías	vivas	vivieras
viviendo	vive	vivió	vivía	vivirá	viviría	viva	viviera
(living)	vivimos	vivimos	vivíamos	viviremos	viviríamos	vivamos	viviéramos
vivido (lived)	vivís	vivisteis	vivíais	viviréis	viviríais	viváis	viviereis
	viven	vivieron	vivían	vivirán	vivirían	vivan	vivieran

Regular verbs, perfect tenses[†]

INDICATIVE							
Present Perfect		Past Perfect		Future Perfect		Conditional Perfect	
he	hablado	había	hablado	habré	hablado	habría	hablado
has	comido	habías	comido	habrás	comido	habrías	comido
ha	vivido	había	vivido	habrá	vivido	habría	vivido
hemos		habíamos		habremos		habríamos	
habéis		habíais		habréis		habríais	
han		habían		habrán		habrían	

SUBJUNCTIVE			
Present Perfect		Past Perfect	
haya	hablado	hubiera	hablado
hayas	comido	hubieras	comido
haya	vivido	hubiera	vivido
hayamos		hubiéramos	
hayáis		hubierais	
hayan		hubieran	

[†]As in English, perfect tenses in Spanish use the helping verb *haber* (to have). However, to indicate possession Spanish uses the verb *tener* (to have).

distracciones

Some common irregular verbs, simple tenses

Infinitive & Participles	INDICATIVE						SUBJUNCTIVE	
	Present	Preterit	Imperfect	Future	Conditional		Present	Past
estar (*to be*)	estoy	estuve	estaba	estaré	estaría		esté	estuviera
	estás	estuviste	estabas	estarás	estarías		estés	estuvieras
	está	estuvo	estaba	estará	estaría		esté	estuviera
estando (*being*)	estamos	estuvimos	estábamos	estaremos	estaríamos		estemos	estuviéramos
estado (*been*)	estáis	estuvisteis	estabais	estaréis	estaríais		estéis	estuvierais
	están	estuvieron	estaban	estarán	estarían		estén	estuvieran
dar (*to give*)	doy	di	daba	daré	daría		dé	diera
	das	diste	dabas	darás	darías		des	dieras
	da	dio	daba	dará	daría		dé	diera
dando (*giving*)	damos	dimos	dábamos	daremos	daríamos		demos	diéramos
dado (*given*)	dais	disteis	dabais	daréis	daríais		deis	dierais
	dan	dieron	daban	darán	darían		den	dieran
hacer (*to do, to make*)	hago	hice	hacía	haré	haría		haga	hiciera
	haces	hiciste	hacías	harás	harías		hagas	hicieras
	hace	hizo	hacía	hará	haría		haga	hiciera
haciendo (*making*)	hacemos	hicimos	hacíamos	haremos	haríamos		hagamos	hiciéramos
hecho (*made*)	hacéis	hicisteis	hacíais	haréis	haríais		hagáis	hiciereis
	hacen	hicieron	hacían	harán	harían		hagan	hicieran

Verb Conjugation Tables

ir (to go) · yendo (going) · ido (gone)

	Present	Preterit	Imperfect	Future	Conditional	Pres. Subj.	Past Subj.
	voy	fui	iba	iré	iría	vaya	fuera
	vas	fuiste	ibas	irás	irías	vayas	fueras
	va	fue	iba	irá	iría	vaya	fuera
	vamos	fuimos	íbamos	iremos	iríamos	vayamos	fuéramos
	vais	fuisteis	ibais	iréis	iríais	vayáis	fuerais
	van	fueron	iban	irán	irían	vayan	fueran

ser (to be) · siendo (being) · sido (been)

	Present	Preterit	Imperfect	Future	Conditional	Pres. Subj.	Past Subj.
	soy	fui*	era	seré	sería	sea	fuera
	eres	fuiste	eras	serás	serías	seas	fueras
	es	fue	era	será	sería	sea	fuera
	somos	fuimos	éramos	seremos	seríamos	seamos	fuéramos
	sois	fuisteis	erais	seréis	seríais	seáis	fuerais
	son	fueron	eran	serán	serían	sean	fueran

venir (to come) · viniendo (coming) · venido (come)

	Present	Preterit	Imperfect	Future	Conditional	Pres. Subj.	Past Subj.
	vengo	vine	venía	vendré	vendría	venga	viniera
	vienes	viniste	venías	vendrás	vendrías	vengas	vinieras
	viene	vino	venía	vendrá	vendría	venga	viniera
	venimos	vinimos	veníamos	vendremos	vendríamos	vengamos	viniéramos
	venís	vinisteis	veníais	vendréis	vendríais	vengáis	viniereis
	vienen	vinieron	venían	vendrán	vendrían	vengan	vinieran

---

*The verbs *ser* and *ir* share the preterit and past subjunctive tenses; context determines which verb is being used.

Verbs, Tenses, and Moods

Ser vs. Estar

English translates both the verb *ser* and the verb *estar* as "to be." However, in Spanish they have very different meanings. *Ser* is used to talk about essences (aspects that are perceived as being inherent to or definitive of the subject) and about time. *Estar* is used to talk about states (aspects or conditions that are merely circumstantial to the subject) and about location (space). Compare the following sentences:

Pedro **es** un tipo simpático pero hoy **está** enojado.	*Pedro is a nice guy but today he is angry.*
Son las dos y María todavía **está** dormida.*	*It is two o'clock and María is still asleep.*
La casa que **está** en esa colina **es** amarilla.	*The house that is on that hill is yellow.*
La fiesta **fue** en la casa que **está** en venta.‡	*The party was at the house that is for sale.*

The verb *estar* is used in combination with a gerund to form progressive tenses:

Estoy escribiendo en la computadora.	*I am writing on the computer.*
Estábamos pensando en llamarte.	*We were thinking about calling you.*

---

*States can be permanent. In Spanish, death is considered a state: Las plantas de mi casa **están** muertas (*My house plants are dead*).

‡Since events are not equivalent to their location, the verb *ser* is used to talk about parties and ceremonies in general: la boda **será** en la catedral (*The wedding will be in the cathedral*).

Preterit vs. Imperfect

The preterit tense is used when a past action is considered singular and definitely concluded:

Pasé un mes en Madrid el año pasado. — *I spent a month in Madrid last year.*

Fue entonces cuando **conocí** a Juan. — *It was then that I met Juan.*

The imperfect tense is used for recurring actions in the past or actions which happened over an indefinite period of time in the past:

Antes, **iba** a Madrid cada año. — *Before, I used to go to Madrid every year.*

En esa época, Juan **estudiaba** leyes. — *At the time, Juan studied (was studying) law.*

The preterit and the imperfect are often combined in a sentence to emphasize certain events (preterit) over others that provide context or serve as backdrop (imperfect):

Decidí comer mientras te **esperaba**. — *I decided to eat lunch while I waited (was waiting) for you.*

Llovía cuando **llegó** el avión. — *It was raining when the plane arrived.*

Subjunctive mood

In Spanish, the subjunctive mood is used to express possibility, uncertainty, and empathy. When speaking about actions that happen in the present, happened in the past, or will happen in the future, the indicative mood is used. For talking about actions which may (or may not) happen, or may (or may not) have happened, the subjunctive mood is used. In general, the subjunctive is used to talk about situations that are beyond the control of a sentence's primary subject. For instance, we may say that it is important, necessary even, for drivers to come to a full stop at a stop sign which, however, does not guarantee that they will. Likewise, even if Juan wanted Pedro to lend him money, Pedro might have refused. Finally, a person may feel sorry about another's tragedy, but be unable to do anything to change it. Consider the following examples:

Es posible que **vaya** a México en verano.
It is possible that I will go to Mexico in the summer.

Es importante (necesario) que los conductores **respeten** las señales de tránsito.
It is important (necessary) that drivers respect traffic signals.

Juan quería que Pedro le **prestara** dinero.
Juan wanted Pedro to lend him money.

Siento que **hayas perdido** tu vuelo.
I am sorry that you (have) missed your flight.

Note that when a single subject is involved in the action there is no need to introduce a subjunctive clause; the verb in the infinitive is used in the main clause instead. Compare the following sentences:

Quiero que (tú) **aprendas** español. *I want you to learn Spanish.*

Quiero **aprender** español.   *I want to learn Spanish.*

Commands and requests

	Affirmative commands	Negative commands
Informal commands	habla (*talk*) come (*eat*) siénta**te** (*sit down*)	no hables (*don't talk*) no comas (*don't eat*) no **te** sientes (*don't sit down*)
Formal commands (requests)	hable (*talk*) coma (*eat*) siénte**se** (*sit down*)	no hable (*don't talk*) no coma (*don't eat*) no **se** siente (*don't sit down*)

Commands can be affirmative or negative. In Spanish they can also be formal or informal. Informal commands are directed at someone whom the speaker would address as *"tú"* (a child, a family member, a good friend, etc.). On the other hand, formal commands are directed towards someone who would be addressed as *"usted"* such as an elder, a teacher, an officer, the president, a new acquaintance, etc. (see PRONOUNS section beginning on p. 203).

Prepositions

Prepositions in any language can seem arbitrary—in English people can ride **in** a car or **on** a bus. However, there are a few general guidelines for using the most common prepositions in Spanish:

a *(to)* conveys the sense of going toward something. Actions such as going somewhere, beginning or learning something, and giving something to someone use the preposition **a**:

Vamos **a** la escuela para empezar **a** aprender **a** hablar español.
Let's go to school in order to begin learning to speak Spanish.

de *(of, from)* conveys the sense of coming or stemming from somewhere. The preposition **de** can express provenance, origin, material, and belonging:

La madera **de** la mesa **de** madera **de** Juan viene **de** la selva **de** Guatemala.
The wood that Juan's wooden table is made of comes from the jungle of Guatemala.

en *(in, on, at)* expresses location in general:

En la universidad, los libros están **en** repisas **en** la biblioteca.
At the university, the books are on shelves in the library.

con *(with)* expresses addition, instrumentality, and accompaniment:

Me gusta comer fresas **con** crema **con** una cuchara **con** mis amigos.
I like to eat strawberries with cream with a spoon with my friends.

para *(for, to, in order to, by)* points toward the end point of an action. **Para** specifies the recipient or the purpose of an action, as well as a direction, a destination, or a deadline.

El regalo **para** mi mamá estará listo **para** mañana; es una caja **para** guardar sus joyas.

The present for my mom will be ready by tomorrow; it's a box for storing her jewelry.

por (*for, because of, around, through, by*). **Por** indicates the cause or the reason behind an action, as well as motion, passage, means, and exchange.

Vamos a hacer un viaje **por** barco **por** el Caribe **por** tres semanas; pagué mil dólares **por** él.

We're going on a trip around the Caribbean by boat for three weeks; I paid $1,000 dollars for it.

Note that the use of prepositions in English doesn't always match Spanish use. In some cases, English needs a preposition where Spanish does not:

Juan se enamoró **de** María.	*Juan fell in love **with** Mary.*
Puedes contar **con** nosotros.	*You can count **on** us.*
Estoy buscando algo especial.	*I'm looking **for** something special.*

A CATALOG OF SELECTED DOVER
BOOKS IN ALL FIELDS OF INTEREST

100 BEST-LOVED POEMS, Edited by Philip Smith. "The Passionate Shepherd to His Love," "Shall I compare thee to a summer's day?" "Death, be not proud," "The Raven," "The Road Not Taken," plus works by Blake, Wordsworth, Byron, Shelley, Keats, many others. 96pp. 5³⁄₁₆ x 8¼. 0-486-28553-7

100 SMALL HOUSES OF THE THIRTIES, Brown-Blodgett Company. Exterior photographs and floor plans for 100 charming structures. Illustrations of models accompanied by descriptions of interiors, color schemes, closet space, and other amenities. 200 illustrations. 112pp. 8⅜ x 11. 0-486-44131-8

1000 TURN-OF-THE-CENTURY HOUSES: With Illustrations and Floor Plans, Herbert C. Chivers. Reproduced from a rare edition, this showcase of homes ranges from cottages and bungalows to sprawling mansions. Each house is meticulously illustrated and accompanied by complete floor plans. 256pp. 9⅜ x 12¼.
0-486-45596-3

101 GREAT AMERICAN POEMS, Edited by The American Poetry & Literacy Project. Rich treasury of verse from the 19th and 20th centuries includes works by Edgar Allan Poe, Robert Frost, Walt Whitman, Langston Hughes, Emily Dickinson, T. S. Eliot, other notables. 96pp. 5³⁄₁₆ x 8¼. 0-486-40158-8

101 GREAT SAMURAI PRINTS, Utagawa Kuniyoshi. Kuniyoshi was a master of the warrior woodblock print — and these 18th-century illustrations represent the pinnacle of his craft. Full-color portraits of renowned Japanese samurais pulse with movement, passion, and remarkably fine detail. 112pp. 8⅜ x 11. 0-486-46523-3

ABC OF BALLET, Janet Grosser. Clearly worded, abundantly illustrated little guide defines basic ballet-related terms: arabesque, battement, pas de chat, relevé, sissonne, many others. Pronunciation guide included. Excellent primer. 48pp. 4³⁄₁₆ x 5¾.
0-486-40871-X

ACCESSORIES OF DRESS: An Illustrated Encyclopedia, Katherine Lester and Bess Viola Oerke. Illustrations of hats, veils, wigs, cravats, shawls, shoes, gloves, and other accessories enhance an engaging commentary that reveals the humor and charm of the many-sided story of accessorized apparel. 644 figures and 59 plates. 608pp. 6 ⅛ x 9¼.
0-486-43378-1

ADVENTURES OF HUCKLEBERRY FINN, Mark Twain. Join Huck and Jim as their boyhood adventures along the Mississippi River lead them into a world of excitement, danger, and self-discovery. Humorous narrative, lyrical descriptions of the Mississippi valley, and memorable characters. 224pp. 5³⁄₁₆ x 8¼. 0-486-28061-6

ALICE STARMORE'S BOOK OF FAIR ISLE KNITTING, Alice Starmore. A noted designer from the region of Scotland's Fair Isle explores the history and techniques of this distinctive, stranded-color knitting style and provides copious illustrated instructions for 14 original knitwear designs. 208pp. 8⅜ x 10⅞. 0-486-47218-3

Browse over 9,000 books at www.doverpublications.com

ALICE'S ADVENTURES IN WONDERLAND, Lewis Carroll. Beloved classic about a little girl lost in a topsy-turvy land and her encounters with the White Rabbit, March Hare, Mad Hatter, Cheshire Cat, and other delightfully improbable characters. 42 illustrations by Sir John Tenniel. 96pp. 5³⁄₁₆ x 8¼.   0-486-27543-4

AMERICA'S LIGHTHOUSES: An Illustrated History, Francis Ross Holland. Profusely illustrated fact-filled survey of American lighthouses since 1716. Over 200 stations — East, Gulf, and West coasts, Great Lakes, Hawaii, Alaska, Puerto Rico, the Virgin Islands, and the Mississippi and St. Lawrence Rivers. 240pp. 8 x 10¾.

0-486-25576-X

AN ENCYCLOPEDIA OF THE VIOLIN, Alberto Bachmann. Translated by Frederick H. Martens. Introduction by Eugene Ysaye. First published in 1925, this renowned reference remains unsurpassed as a source of essential information, from construction and evolution to repertoire and technique. Includes a glossary and 73 illustrations. 496pp. 6⅛ x 9¼.   0-486-46618-3

ANIMALS: 1,419 Copyright-Free Illustrations of Mammals, Birds, Fish, Insects, etc., Selected by Jim Harter. Selected for its visual impact and ease of use, this outstanding collection of wood engravings presents over 1,000 species of animals in extremely lifelike poses. Includes mammals, birds, reptiles, amphibians, fish, insects, and other invertebrates. 284pp. 9 x 12.   0-486-23766-4

THE ANNALS, Tacitus. Translated by Alfred John Church and William Jackson Brodribb. This vital chronicle of Imperial Rome, written by the era's great historian, spans A.D. 14-68 and paints incisive psychological portraits of major figures, from Tiberius to Nero. 416pp. 5³⁄₁₆ x 8¼.   0-486-45236-0

ANTIGONE, Sophocles. Filled with passionate speeches and sensitive probing of moral and philosophical issues, this powerful and often-performed Greek drama reveals the grim fate that befalls the children of Oedipus. Footnotes. 64pp. 5³⁄₁₆ x 8 ¼.   0-486-27804-2

ART DECO DECORATIVE PATTERNS IN FULL COLOR, Christian Stoll. Reprinted from a rare 1910 portfolio, 160 sensuous and exotic images depict a breathtaking array of florals, geometrics, and abstracts — all elegant in their stark simplicity. 64pp. 8⅜ x 11.   0-486-44862-2

THE ARTHUR RACKHAM TREASURY: 86 Full-Color Illustrations, Arthur Rackham. Selected and Edited by Jeff A. Menges. A stunning treasury of 86 full-page plates span the famed English artist's career, from *Rip Van Winkle* (1905) to masterworks such as *Undine, A Midsummer Night's Dream,* and *Wind in the Willows* (1939). 96pp. 8⅜ x 11.

0-486-44685-9

THE AUTHENTIC GILBERT & SULLIVAN SONGBOOK, W. S. Gilbert and A. S. Sullivan. The most comprehensive collection available, this songbook includes selections from every one of Gilbert and Sullivan's light operas. Ninety-two numbers are presented uncut and unedited, and in their original keys. 410pp. 9 x 12.

0-486-23482-7

THE AWAKENING, Kate Chopin. First published in 1899, this controversial novel of a New Orleans wife's search for love outside a stifling marriage shocked readers. Today, it remains a first-rate narrative with superb characterization. New introductory Note. 128pp. 5³⁄₁₆ x 8¼.   0-486-27786-0

BASIC DRAWING, Louis Priscilla. Beginning with perspective, this commonsense manual progresses to the figure in movement, light and shade, anatomy, drapery, composition, trees and landscape, and outdoor sketching. Black-and-white illustrations throughout. 128pp. 8⅜ x 11.   0-486-45815-6

Browse over 9,000 books at www.doverpublications.com

THE BATTLES THAT CHANGED HISTORY, Fletcher Pratt. Historian profiles 16 crucial conflicts, ancient to modern, that changed the course of Western civilization. Gripping accounts of battles led by Alexander the Great, Joan of Arc, Ulysses S. Grant, other commanders. 27 maps. 352pp. 5⅜ x 8½. 0-486-41129-X

BEETHOVEN'S LETTERS, Ludwig van Beethoven. Edited by Dr. A. C. Kalischer. Features 457 letters to fellow musicians, friends, greats, patrons, and literary men. Reveals musical thoughts, quirks of personality, insights, and daily events. Includes 15 plates. 410pp. 5⅜ x 8½. 0-486-22769-3

BERNICE BOBS HER HAIR AND OTHER STORIES, F. Scott Fitzgerald. This brilliant anthology includes 6 of Fitzgerald's most popular stories: "The Diamond as Big as the Ritz," the title tale, "The Offshore Pirate," "The Ice Palace," "The Jelly Bean," and "May Day." 176pp. 5⅜ x 8½. 0-486-47049-0

BESLER'S BOOK OF FLOWERS AND PLANTS: 73 Full-Color Plates from Hortus Eystettensis, 1613, Basilius Besler. Here is a selection of magnificent plates from the *Hortus Eystettensis,* which vividly illustrated and identified the plants, flowers, and trees that thrived in the legendary German garden at Eichstätt. 80pp. 8⅜ x 11.
0-486-46005-3

THE BOOK OF KELLS, Edited by Blanche Cirker. Painstakingly reproduced from a rare facsimile edition, this volume contains full-page decorations, portraits, illustrations, plus a sampling of textual leaves with exquisite calligraphy and ornamentation. 32 full-color illustrations. 32pp. 9⅜ x 12¼. 0-486-24345-1

THE BOOK OF THE CROSSBOW: With an Additional Section on Catapults and Other Siege Engines, Ralph Payne-Gallwey. Fascinating study traces history and use of crossbow as military and sporting weapon, from Middle Ages to modern times. Also covers related weapons: balistas, catapults, Turkish bows, more. Over 240 illustrations. 400pp. 7¼ x 10⅛. 0-486-28720-3

THE BUNGALOW BOOK: Floor Plans and Photos of 112 Houses, 1910, Henry L. Wilson. Here are 112 of the most popular and economic blueprints of the early 20th century — plus an illustration or photograph of each completed house. A wonderful time capsule that still offers a wealth of valuable insights. 160pp. 8⅜ x 11.
0-486-45104-6

THE CALL OF THE WILD, Jack London. A classic novel of adventure, drawn from London's own experiences as a Klondike adventurer, relating the story of a heroic dog caught in the brutal life of the Alaska Gold Rush. Note. 64pp. 5³⁄₁₆ x 8¼.
0-486-26472-6

CANDIDE, Voltaire. Edited by Francois-Marie Arouet. One of the world's great satires since its first publication in 1759. Witty, caustic skewering of romance, science, philosophy, religion, government — nearly all human ideals and institutions. 112pp. 5³⁄₁₆ x 8¼. 0-486-26689-3

CELEBRATED IN THEIR TIME: Photographic Portraits from the George Grantham Bain Collection, Edited by Amy Pastan. With an Introduction by Michael Carlebach. Remarkable portrait gallery features 112 rare images of Albert Einstein, Charlie Chaplin, the Wright Brothers, Henry Ford, and other luminaries from the worlds of politics, art, entertainment, and industry. 128pp. 8⅜ x 11. 0-486-46754-6

CHARIOTS FOR APOLLO: The NASA History of Manned Lunar Spacecraft to 1969, Courtney G. Brooks, James M. Grimwood, and Loyd S. Swenson, Jr. This illustrated history by a trio of experts is the definitive reference on the Apollo spacecraft and lunar modules. It traces the vehicles' design, development, and operation in space. More than 100 photographs and illustrations. 576pp. 6¾ x 9¼. 0-486-46756-2

A CHRISTMAS CAROL, Charles Dickens. This engrossing tale relates Ebenezer Scrooge's ghostly journeys through Christmases past, present, and future and his ultimate transformation from a harsh and grasping old miser to a charitable and compassionate human being. 80pp. 5³⁄₁₆ x 8¼. 0-486-26865-9

COMMON SENSE, Thomas Paine. First published in January of 1776, this highly influential landmark document clearly and persuasively argued for American separation from Great Britain and paved the way for the Declaration of Independence. 64pp. 5³⁄₁₆ x 8¼. 0-486-29602-4

THE COMPLETE SHORT STORIES OF OSCAR WILDE, Oscar Wilde. Complete texts of "The Happy Prince and Other Tales," "A House of Pomegranates," "Lord Arthur Savile's Crime and Other Stories," "Poems in Prose," and "The Portrait of Mr. W. H." 208pp. 5³⁄₁₆ x 8¼. 0-486-45216-6

COMPLETE SONNETS, William Shakespeare. Over 150 exquisite poems deal with love, friendship, the tyranny of time, beauty's evanescence, death, and other themes in language of remarkable power, precision, and beauty. Glossary of archaic terms. 80pp. 5³⁄₁₆ x 8¼. 0-486-26686-9

THE COUNT OF MONTE CRISTO: Abridged Edition, Alexandre Dumas. Falsely accused of treason, Edmond Dantès is imprisoned in the bleak Chateau d'If. After a hair-raising escape, he launches an elaborate plot to extract a bitter revenge against those who betrayed him. 448pp. 5³⁄₁₆ x 8¼. 0-486-45643-9

CRAFTSMAN BUNGALOWS: Designs from the Pacific Northwest, Yoho & Merritt. This reprint of a rare catalog, showcasing the charming simplicity and cozy style of Craftsman bungalows, is filled with photos of completed homes, plus floor plans and estimated costs. An indispensable resource for architects, historians, and illustrators. 112pp. 10 x 7. 0-486-46875-5

CRAFTSMAN BUNGALOWS: 59 Homes from "The Craftsman," Edited by Gustav Stickley. Best and most attractive designs from Arts and Crafts Movement publication — 1903–1916 — includes sketches, photographs of homes, floor plans, descriptive text. 128pp. 8¼ x 11. 0-486-25829-7

CRIME AND PUNISHMENT, Fyodor Dostoyevsky. Translated by Constance Garnett. Supreme masterpiece tells the story of Raskolnikov, a student tormented by his own thoughts after he murders an old woman. Overwhelmed by guilt and terror, he confesses and goes to prison. 480pp. 5³⁄₁₆ x 8¼. 0-486-41587-2

THE DECLARATION OF INDEPENDENCE AND OTHER GREAT DOCUMENTS OF AMERICAN HISTORY: 1775-1865, Edited by John Grafton. Thirteen compelling and influential documents: Henry's "Give Me Liberty or Give Me Death," Declaration of Independence, The Constitution, Washington's First Inaugural Address, The Monroe Doctrine, The Emancipation Proclamation, Gettysburg Address, more. 64pp. 5³⁄₁₆ x 8¼. 0-486-41124-9

THE DESERT AND THE SOWN: Travels in Palestine and Syria, Gertrude Bell. "The female Lawrence of Arabia," Gertrude Bell wrote captivating, perceptive accounts of her travels in the Middle East. This intriguing narrative, accompanied by 160 photos, traces her 1905 sojourn in Lebanon, Syria, and Palestine. 368pp. 5⅜ x 8½.
0-486-46876-3

A DOLL'S HOUSE, Henrik Ibsen. Ibsen's best-known play displays his genius for realistic prose drama. An expression of women's rights, the play climaxes when the central character, Nora, rejects a smothering marriage and life in "a doll's house." 80pp. 5³⁄₁₆ x 8¼. 0-486-27062-9

DOOMED SHIPS: Great Ocean Liner Disasters, William H. Miller, Jr. Nearly 200 photographs, many from private collections, highlight tales of some of the vessels whose pleasure cruises ended in catastrophe: the *Morro Castle, Normandie, Andrea Doria, Europa,* and many others. 128pp. 8⅞ x 11¾.   0-486-45366-9

THE DORÉ BIBLE ILLUSTRATIONS, Gustave Doré. Detailed plates from the Bible: the Creation scenes, Adam and Eve, horrifying visions of the Flood, the battle sequences with their monumental crowds, depictions of the life of Jesus, 241 plates in all. 241pp. 9 x 12.   0-486-23004-X

DRAWING DRAPERY FROM HEAD TO TOE, Cliff Young. Expert guidance on how to draw shirts, pants, skirts, gloves, hats, and coats on the human figure, including folds in relation to the body, pull and crush, action folds, creases, more. Over 200 drawings. 48pp. 8¼ x 11.   0-486-45591-2

DUBLINERS, James Joyce. A fine and accessible introduction to the work of one of the 20th century's most influential writers, this collection features 15 tales, including a masterpiece of the short-story genre, "The Dead." 160pp. 5³⁄₁₆ x 8¼.

0-486-26870-5

EASY-TO-MAKE POP-UPS, Joan Irvine. Illustrated by Barbara Reid. Dozens of wonderful ideas for three-dimensional paper fun — from holiday greeting cards with moving parts to a pop-up menagerie. Easy-to-follow, illustrated instructions for more than 30 projects. 299 black-and-white illustrations. 96pp. 8⅜ x 11.

0-486-44622-0

EASY-TO-MAKE STORYBOOK DOLLS: A "Novel" Approach to Cloth Dollmaking, Sherralyn St. Clair. Favorite fictional characters come alive in this unique beginner's dollmaking guide. Includes patterns for Pollyanna, Dorothy from *The Wonderful Wizard of Oz,* Mary of *The Secret Garden,* plus easy-to-follow instructions, 263 black-and-white illustrations, and an 8-page color insert. 112pp. 8¼ x 11.   0-486-47360-0

EINSTEIN'S ESSAYS IN SCIENCE, Albert Einstein. Speeches and essays in accessible, everyday language profile influential physicists such as Niels Bohr and Isaac Newton. They also explore areas of physics to which the author made major contributions. 128pp. 5 x 8.   0-486-47011-3

EL DORADO: Further Adventures of the Scarlet Pimpernel, Baroness Orczy. A popular sequel to *The Scarlet Pimpernel,* this suspenseful story recounts the Pimpernel's attempts to rescue the Dauphin from imprisonment during the French Revolution. An irresistible blend of intrigue, period detail, and vibrant characterizations. 352pp. 5³⁄₁₆ x 8¼.   0-486-44026-5

ELEGANT SMALL HOMES OF THE TWENTIES: 99 Designs from a Competition, Chicago Tribune. Nearly 100 designs for five- and six-room houses feature New England and Southern colonials, Normandy cottages, stately Italianate dwellings, and other fascinating snapshots of American domestic architecture of the 1920s. 112pp. 9 x 12.   0-486-46910-7

THE ELEMENTS OF STYLE: The Original Edition, William Strunk, Jr. This is the book that generations of writers have relied upon for timeless advice on grammar, diction, syntax, and other essentials. In concise terms, it identifies the principal requirements of proper style and common errors. 64pp. 5⅜ x 8½.   0-486-44798-7

THE ELUSIVE PIMPERNEL, Baroness Orczy. Robespierre's revolutionaries find their wicked schemes thwarted by the heroic Pimpernel — Sir Percival Blakeney. In this thrilling sequel, Chauvelin devises a plot to eliminate the Pimpernel and his wife. 272pp. 5³⁄₁₆ x 8¼.   0-486-45464-9